Life's
too short
to
Chop
Onions

Life's too short to Chop Onions

99 dishes to make when you'd rather be doing something else

KITTY GREENWALD

Reader's Digest

The Reader's Digest Association, Inc.
Pleasantville, New York

A READER'S DIGEST BOOK

This edition published by The Reader's Digest Association, Inc.
by arrangement with Toucan Books Ltd.

FOR TOUCAN BOOKS
Project Designer Clare Marshall
Project Editor Theresa Bebbington
Managing Editor Ellen Dupont
Proofreader Constance Novis
Indexer Jackie Brind
Illustrations kja-artists.com
Cover Illustration Shutterstock: Maljuk

FOR READER'S DIGEST
U.S. Project Editor Kim Casey
Copy Editor Jen Graham
Project Designer Jennifer Tokarski
Senior Art Director George McKeon
Executive Editor, Trade Publishing Dolores York
Associate Publisher Rosanne McManus
President and Publisher, Trade Publishing Harold Clarke

Library of Congress Cataloging-in-Publication Data
Greenwald, Kitty, 1978-
Life's too short to chop onions : 99 dishes to make when you'd rather be doing
something else / Kitty Greenwald.
p. cm.
ISBN 978-1-60652-124-3
1. Quick and easy cookery. I. Title.
TX833.5.G743 2010
641.5'55--dc22   2009047914

We are committed to both the quality of our products and the service we provide
to our customers. We value your comments, so please feel free to contact us.

The Reader's Digest Association, Inc.
Adult Trade Publishing
Reader's Digest Road
Pleasantville, NY 10570-7000

For more Reader's Digest products and information, visit our website:
www.rd.com (in the United States)

Printed in China
1 3 5 7 9 10 8 6 4 2

Contents

Introduction

Hey, you with the takeout menu! Step away from the
phone. There's a secret inside this little book that I'd like
to share with you. Cooking is not that hard. That's right.
I said it! And my book, *Life's Too Short to Chop Onions*,
will prove it.

I know that you don't see the kitchen as a refuge or find
cooking to be relaxing. That's fine. There are other places for
that (the massage table, for starters). Now, it's true, I love to
cook. But we are going to get along just fine anyway. In my
family, I'm in the minority. Most of my nearest and dearest
do not (gasp!) like to cook. That doesn't mean they can't be
good at it. And I hate to sound like your first-grade teacher
here, but it doesn't mean you shouldn't try.

So why bother? Well there are plenty of reasons and
common ones include duty (funny how those kids keep
demanding to be fed!), health (preservatives, fats, and sugars
really aren't great for the waistline), and financial sense
(the cost of eating out and ordering in can hurt more than
a burned finger). Since these reasons are all legitimate, a
cookbook with simple, wholesome, easy recipes seems
long overdue. So here it is, direct from me to you.

Life's Too Short to Chop Onions keeps the kitchen-phobic
person in mind from the first page to the last. It begins with
explanations of basic techniques and kitchen items and ends
with a list of proposed menus for a range of occasions and

tastes. In between, the book is packed with 99 streamlined recipes with easy-to-follow directions. Over the years, I've learned dishes, techniques, and shortcuts and I'm sharing them with you because I think everyone deserves to eat well without taking too much time to prepare their meals.

You'll find there are suggestions and tips scattered throughout my book. The dishes are tasty enough for a gourmet but made easy enough for those who don't know how to boil an egg. (OK, sorry, I know you know how to do that. You do, right?) As for all your other cookbooks? Stick a fork in 'em! They're done. You're ready for this one. You don't need a giant encyclopedic listing all the recipes under the sun. Instead, you need a book with only enough to satisfy; and 99 recipes is perfect. Let's get started.

Foods to Have Handy

Like your little black dress, keep your basics on hand and you'll be ready for anything.

READY-TO-EAT FOODS

Bread Sliced bread, buns, naan, pita, tortilla—any and all are a must. For long-term storage, put bread in your freezer. When ready to use it, take it out, thaw, and toast.

Cakes, cookies, and ice cream Dessert minus the cooking! Add fruit for freshness.

Cereal Just add milk; granola is also good for baking.

Cheese Brie, cheddar, cream cheese, feta, goat, mozzarella, you name it—all are delicious as a snack or essential in many recipes.

Chicken, rotisserie Invaluable to avoid cooking.

Deli and cured meats Ham and chorizo not only make speedy sandwiches but are often used in recipes.

Jam For toast (a perfect snack for one) or as a quick pie filling.

Nuts Almonds, cashews, peanuts, pecans, and walnuts are quick snacks, easy cocktail nibbles, and used in desserts and salads.

Olives Buy them with their pits—they will have more flavor than pitiful pit-free ones—but use without pits for sauces.

Tuna A meal in waiting.

ALMOST READY-TO-EAT FOODS

The following are either just a few steps away from turning into a dish or essential elements that appear in many dishes.

Beans, canned Cannellini, chickpea, kidney, navy, pinto—keep a variety in your pantry; when ready to use, drain in a colander over a sink, rinse, and drain again.

Chicken broth or stock For quick soups or simmering casseroles.

Couscous A quick-cooking, delicious side.

Eggs Great for a quick omelet or scrambled.

Garlic Adds body and flavor, and easy to prepare (see page 12).

Mayonnaise/mustard From sauces to salads to sandwiches, these spreads are pantry must-haves.

Onions You don't need to chop, but onions are used in too many dishes to ignore altogether, tears or not.

Pasta Keep a variety—tubular (penne, rigatoni), shapes (bow ties, shells), and straight (spaghetti, linguini).

Peas Use frozen ones for the best sweet and fresh flavor.

Potatoes Choose starchy russets for mashing, frying, and baking; waxy round white or red potatoes are better for boiling.

Rice White, brown, or wild.

Sour cream or Greek yogurt Substitute Greek yogurt for sour cream as a healthy alternative.

Tomatoes, canned Whole and crushed; some recipes use the juices, but in others they are drained—pour into a colander over a sink.

PANTRY STAPLES

Herbs, dried Basil, bay, oregano, rosemary, sage, thyme

Honey

Oil Olive and either vegetable or canola

Pepper Ground black and/or peppercorns

Salt

Spices Cayenne, cinnamon, cloves, coriander, cumin, nutmeg, paprika, red pepper flakes, star anise

Sauces Hoisin, oyster, soy, Tabasco, Worcestershire

Sugar Confectioners' (or powdered), granulated, and light brown

Tomato paste

Vinegar Balsamic, red wine, rice wine, white wine

Wine Red and white (good for cooking and for nerves)

Kitchen Equipment

The right kitchen equipment is essential. Why? Simple.
It minimizes the amount of work you need to do.

ESSENTIAL EQUIPMENT

Can and bottle opener

Deep pot A heavy pot with a lid, such as a Dutch oven, is good for stews and soups.

Knives You need a paring knife for making small cuts and trimming, and a long knife with a broad blade for cutting almost everything else. A serrated knife is best for slicing bread and soft fruit and vegetables—think tomatoes—without squishing them.

Long-handled spoons Three is a good number to have and at least one should be wooden because it doesn't conduct heat.

Mixing bowls Small, medium, and large—one of each.

Pot holders or oven mitts A must to prevent burned fingers.

Sauté pan A heavy, large nonstick pan is ideal.

INCREDIBLY USEFUL EQUIPMENT

Baking sheet One is good, plus a cookie sheet (it won't have a rim).

Box grater Good for grating cheese or carrots.

Cake pan Two are enough.

Coffee or spice grinder or mortar and pestle Two pieces of equipment that do the same thing, but a grinder is less work.

Colander To pour out hot water when boiling pasta or veggies.

Deep roasting pan One is all you need to roast a bird.

Electric mixer You could beat cream or butter by hand, but why?

Food processor Lfe's too short to live without a food processor. It chops, mixes, purees, and liquifies at the push of a button.

Garlic press Or just smash and peel as directed on page 12.

Ladle To transfer liquid-y substances, you'll need a ladle (a spoon will take about 500 times longer, and pouring is bound to be messy).

Masher For potatoes or rough purees.

Meat thermometer Stick it in the thickest part of your meat, away from the bone; when it reaches the right temperature, you'll know the meat is cooked through. It makes cooking a roast foolproof.

Microplane grater Good for everything from grating citrus zest (particularly lemons, my favorite) to grating hard cheeses or whole spices, such as nutmeg or cinnamon.

Ovenproof dishes One large and one small dish are essential if you plan to slam the oven door and scram. You can use flameproof ones on the stove-top and transfer it to the oven or broiler.

Plastic storage containers with lids From small to large, shallow to deep for leftovers.

Salad spinner To wash and dry greens (including prewashed ones) or delicate veggies.

Saucepan One or two for smaller portions and sides.

Slotted Spoon If you ever need to remove anything from boiling water—eggs or veggies—a slotted spoon is what you need.

Spatula Two types, one for flipping—think pancakes—and a rubber one for spreading, folding, and scraping. Why make a sauce or dough if you can't scrape it out of the bowl?

Stockpot For boiling pasta and making big, make-ahead portions. (Cook once, serve twice is my advice.)

Strainer For draining rice or separating liquids from solids, such as the drippings of a roast from unwanted herbs to make an easy gravy.

Tongs Handy for turning or grabbing just about anything. Think of these as burn-proof fingers.

Vegetable peeler You could use a small paring knife, but that takes oodles of time, and with a peeler you can also shave things, such as chocolate and cheese.

Food Preparation

Before you begin, here are a few tips that will make your time in the kitchen a lot happier.

WASHING AND PREPPING

Wash and dry all raw fruit and vegetables, even prewashed ones, before using by rinsing under running water. If there is grit or dirt on the food (usually the case with delicate greens and leeks), shake the ingredients in a basin filled with water to dislodge any grit. Repeat until the water is clear. Transfer the vegetables to a colander to dry. If they will be eaten raw, such as salad greens, spin the veggies dry.

PEELING PRODUCE

A vegetable peeler is the easiest way to remove the peel from carrots and potatoes and can even be used for peeling squash, but what about garlic and onions?

- For garlic, if you need it only for flavor, simply smash the clove open and peel. Hold the broad side of a blade on a heavy knife over a clove lying flat on a work surface. Place your free hand on top of the blade and push down quickly—keep your fingers away from the sharp edge. Once the garlic is smashed, remove the clove and discard the skin. To slice whole garlic, first cut off the thickest end with a paring knife to remove the outer skin.

- To quickly peel an onion or shallot, rub off the flaky exterior and slice off the ends. Run your knife down one side, cutting into the outermost layer and remove. If either needs to be sliced, first halve them and then remove the outer layer.

PROCESSING FOOD

You won't want to chop, and that's where a food processor is handy. Add the ingredients to the bowl of the food processor and quickly press the pulse button repeatedly until they're chopped to the desired size. Don't overdo them or you'll end up with mush. If an ingredient is large, you will need to cut it into smaller 2–3-inch (5–7.5-cm) pieces before adding to the processor.

$\mathcal{Introduction}$

HOW TO CORE AND SEED

- To core and seed a bell pepper, lay it on its side and chop off the stem and bottom end and pull out the core. Stand the pepper upright and cut down lengthwise. Lay out the pepper, skin side up, and scrape out the seeds and membrane.

- For a small pepper, such as a jalapeño, make an incision down the length of the side and splay it open. Scrape out the seeds and membrane—if it's a hot one, wear rubber gloves to avoid getting the oil on your hands (and don't rub your eyes!).

- To core a tomato, lay it on its side. Insert the tip of a paring knife at an angle near the uppermost part of the stem end, about 1 inch (2.5 cm) into the tomato. Cut in a sawing motion around the core until you come full circle; remove the core.

CITRUS ZEST AND JUICE

- To grate the zest from citrus fruit, first rinse and dry the fruit. Then grate down to the pith—the bitter white flesh beneath the skin—using a microplane grater.

- For strips of zest, run a vegetable peeler down the length of the citrus. Remove the strip from the dish before serving.

- To get juice out of citrus fruit, remove the zest, if needed, then roll the fruit on a flat surface, pushing down with the palm of your hand to help extract the juice. Cut the fruit in half. Hold it above a strainer with a bowl beneath, cup your fingers beneath, then squeeze so the juice falls through your fingers.

FRESH HERBS

If only the leaves of a fresh woody herb (rosemary or thyme) are needed, pluck them off the sprigs by running your thumb and index finger along the sprig from the thinnest to the thickest part. Don't have fresh herbs? As a rule of thumb, use 1 teaspoon of dry for each tablespoon of fresh. However, the older the herb, the less flavor it will have, so you may need to add more. The safest bet is to add a little and taste, then adjust the seasoning if you feel it needs more.

~ ONE ~

Shop and serve!

Some people say, "If you can't stand the heat, get out of the kitchen." Well, I say, "If you can't stand the heat, shut off the oven and make something else!" You don't need to start dripping in sweat—from the high temps or the stress. It's time to step away from the oven and create dishes you really want to eat. And they're right here in this chapter, just waiting to make your life easier.

Other benefits? No trips to the emergency room, calls to the fire department, or trying to explain the original identity of a blackened mass. You have better things to do. And I know you can get your warm glow from somewhere else—maybe from that bottle of wine you just uncorked in celebration of your first successful no-oven meal.

Zesty Olives

Olives are teeming with antioxidants. Who doesn't love a recipe that keeps you young?

Prep & cook time, plus marinating time Serves 4–6

2½ cups (435 g) black or green olives, with pits
¼ **teaspoon cumin seeds**
¼ **teaspoon fennel seeds**
2 **1-inch (2.5-cm) strips of orange peel**
1 **bay leaf**
1 **clove garlic, smashed and peeled**
2 **tablespoons olive oil**

1. Rinse the olives under cold running water. Taste an olive to check for saltiness. If necessary, soak the olives in cold water for about 5 minutes to remove excess salt, then drain them in a colander.

2. Crush the cumin and fennel seeds in a spice or coffee grinder or with a mortar and pestle.

3. Put the olives, cumin and fennel seeds, orange peel, bay leaf, and garlic in a bowl. Add the olive oil and toss to combine. Marinate the olives for at least 30 minutes. The longer they marinate, the more the flavors will infuse.

NO MORTAR AND PESTLE?

I guess a coffee or spice grinder is probably out of the question, too. That's OK: Instead, reach for something heavy—a rolling pin, mallet, or even a heavy pan will do—and wrap the seeds inside a clean dish towel. Now give the towel some good whacks until the seeds are finely crushed.

Marinated Mozzarella

Creamy mozzarella, salty capers, and sweet basil are as natural as Chanel and Jackie O. This recipe is so tasty, you'll think the presidential staff made it for you!

Prep & cook time, plus marinating time **5 min** | Serves 4–6

2 **1-inch (2.5-cm) strips of lemon peel**
1 **tablespoon drained and roughly chopped capers**
16 **ounces (450 g) bocconcini (small, fresh mozzarella balls)**
2 **tablespoons roughly chopped fresh oregano**
2 **tablespoons roughly chopped fresh basil**
¼ **cup (60 ml) olive oil**
Salt and ground black pepper

1 Combine all of the ingredients in a medium mixing bowl and toss to coat.

2 Let the mozzarella mixture stand at room temperature for at least 30 minutes before serving.

Swap It!
No bocconcini available in your local supermarket? No problem: Simply swap it for a 16-ounce (450-g) ball of mozzarella instead. However, be sure to buy the fresh kind packed in water—steer away from the vacuum-sealed type, which isn't as soft or tasty. Slice the ball up into slices and you're good to go.

Go Dippy

An addictive dip that keeps well and can easily be repurposed. What's not to like?

Prep & cook time 15 min | Serves 4–6

1½ cups (350 g) plain, whole-milk Greek yogurt
¾ cup (175 g) mayonnaise
Juice and grated zest of 1 lemon
¼ cup (15 g) chopped, mixed fresh herbs (chives, parsley, basil, oregano, tarragon, and/or mint)
Salt and ground black pepper

FOR THE CRUDITÉS
1 bunch of radishes
6 celery stalks
2 medium zucchini or cucumbers
3 carrots

1 In a small bowl, combine the yogurt, mayonnaise, lemon juice and zest, and herbs. Season with salt and pepper.

2 Halve the radishes and remove any discolored leaves. Cut the celery stalks crosswise into 3-inch (7.5-cm) spears. Halve the zucchini or cucumbers lengthwise, slice crosswise into 3-inch (7.5-cm) sections, then slice lengthwise into ½-inch (1-cm)-wide spears. Repeat with the carrots. Serve the dip alongside the crudités.

SECOND LIFE

This dip is too good for serving with only crudités. Be more adventurous and try it with salmon (see page 54), roasted chicken, baked or boiled potatoes, or roasted vegetables. The only cream it shouldn't replace? Your moisturizer.

No-Chop Guac

South of the border, avocado is the star. Here, it shines.

Prep & cook time Serves 4–6

3   ripe avocados
Juice of I lemon
3   tablespoons olive oil
Salt and ground black pepper

Cut the avocados in half and remove the pits (see page 29). Scoop out the flesh and place in a bowl. Add the lemon juice, oil, and salt and pepper, mash with a fork to mix, and serve.

Goat Cheese to Go

This recipe is easy to assemble—and just as easy to polish off.

Prep & cook time Serves 4–6

⅓   cup (15 g) oil-packed sun-dried tomatoes
6   ounces (170 g) fresh goat cheese log
I   teaspoon dried or I tablespoon fresh thyme
Sliced bread or crackers, to serve

1   Drain the sun-dried tomatoes, reserving the oil. Place in a food processor and pulse until finely chopped. If too thick, add enough oil to make it thick but spreadable. Set aside.

2   Clean the bowl of the food processor. Puree the cheese and herbs until smooth. Place in a serving bowl, top with the tomato mixture, and serve with sliced bread or crackers.

My Favorite Crostini

Top miniature open-faced sandwiches, otherwise known as crostini, with anything you like. Below are—you guessed it—my absolute faves.

Prep & cook time | Serves 4

12 slices baguette, cut on the diagonal, ½-inch (1-cm) thick
¼ cup (60 ml) olive oil
Salt

FOR A SINGLE TOPPING

Fresh ricotta cheese, half a dried fig, and a drizzle of honey and olive oil
Marinated red bell pepper, a piece of basil, and an anchovy
Gorgonzola or other blue cheese, a clementine section or half a pitted date, and a walnut

1 Toast the baguette slices, brush with a little oil, and season with salt to taste.

2 Top each toast with one of the topping combinations. Although choosing one of the combinations for all the toasts is easiest and quickest, a variety of toppings will be more impressive and fun. (Why not top off your wine glass while you're at it?)

> ## Swap It!
> For even quicker mini-sandwiches, spread a little tapenade (olive paste) on sliced bread and top with a basil leaf and piece of prosciutto. Another option is to mash 3 tablespoons of butter at room temperature with 1 tablespoon drained and chopped capers. Spread the mixture over sliced French bread and top with a piece of deli ham.

Smoked Salmon with Mustard Cream

This cocktail party staple is all about shopping and assembling. Turn it into an ultra-quick-and-easy meal by serving it with lightly dressed greens and the cucumber-dill salad on page 24.

Prep & cook time | Serves 4

- ¼   **cup (60 g) crème fraîche or sour cream**
- 2   **tablespoons Dijon mustard**
- 14 **slices dry or rye cocktail bread, or thinly sliced country bread, cut into quarters**
- 4   **ounces (115 g) smoked salmon**
- **Small sprigs of dill to garnish**
- **Lemon wedges to serve (optional)**

1 In a small bowl, mix together the crème fraîche or sour cream and mustard. Evenly spread a small amount of the mixture on each slice of bread.

2 Top with 1 or 2 slices of smoked salmon and garnish with a dill sprig. Serve with lemon wedges, if you like.

What's That?

A French specialty, crème fraîche is a thick cream with a nutty, slightly tangy flavor. Look for it in the refrigerated gourmet section of a large supermarket. However, don't fret if you can't find it. Just use sour cream instead, or mix together equal amounts of sour cream and heavy cream.

Blitz-and-Go Gazpacho

This chop-free version is a must for any tomato fan. Looking to wow a special guy? Tell him it's your homage to football season.

Prep & cook time, plus chilling time   Serves 8

2   **pounds (900 g) ripe tomatoes, cored and quartered**
2   **red bell peppers, cored and seeded**
½   **cucumber, peeled and seeded**
3   **cloves garlic, smashed and peeled**
2   **scallions**
¼   **cup (60 ml) olive oil**
3   **tablespoons sherry vinegar or white wine vinegar**
3   **cups (700 ml) tomato juice (optional)**
Salt and ground black pepper

1 Place the tomatoes in a food processor and puree. Add the remaining vegetables, olive oil, and vinegar to the food processor and puree.

2 Taste the mixture and add the tomato juice, if using (if the tomatoes are fully ripe, the juice won't be needed). Season with salt and pepper to taste.

3 Chill in the refrigerator for at least 1 hour, until serving. (The longer gazpacho stands, the more the flavors develop.) It will keep for 2–3 days in the refrigerator.

WOW FACTOR

To make this soup a superstar, serve it with an array of garnishes, including croutons, oven-crisped prosciutto, chopped, hard-boiled eggs, cucumber, tomatoes, or red bell peppers. Only one, or even none, will also be fine—the soup is great alone.

Adults' Watermelon Soup

Refreshing and unique, this summer soup is a breeze to put together. Bad experience with tequila in your past? Omit it altogether.

Prep & cook time, plus chilling time | Serves 4

2 pounds (900 g) prepared, seedless watermelon chunks
¼ cup (60 ml) heavy cream
1 tablespoon tequila (optional)
4 mint leaves, torn, to garnish (optional)

1. Check for and discard any seeds in the watermelon, then puree the watermelon chunks in a food processor until completely smooth.

2. Put the puree to a bowl and stir in the cream. Add the tequila, if using.

3. Chill in the refrigerator for at least 1 hour. Served well chilled in individual bowls, each garnished with a torn mint leaf, if you like.

Swap It!

If there was a run on chopped-up watermelon in your supermarket, or you want to save some money, buy a whole, small seedless watermelon. Split it open, then scoop out the pulp and discard the rind from one half. Save the unused half for another use. Watermelon eating contest, anyone?

Cucumber-Dill Salad

A salad, garnish, relish, or whatever you like, this perky salad is also a perfect side to temper spicy foods. Try it with chicken, fish, or lamb, or eat it plain with pita or naan.

Prep & cook time 15 min  | Serves 4

1 **English cucumber or 2 regular cucumbers**
1 **clove garlic**
2 **tablespoons finely chopped fresh dill**
1½ **cups (350 g) plain, whole-milk Greek yogurt**
Juice of ¼ lemon
Pinch of cayenne
Salt and ground black pepper

1 Halve the cucumber lengthwise. Running the tip of a spoon down the length of the cucumber, scoop out the seeds and discard them. Slice the cucumber into ¹/₄-inch (5-mm) semicircles.

2 Smash the garlic with the back of your knife and finely chop.

3 Whisk together the garlic, chopped dill, yogurt, lemon juice, and cayenne in a mixing bowl.

4 Add the cucumber slices to the yogurt mixture and toss together to combine. Season with salt and pepper to taste and serve immediately.

SAVE IT FOR LATER

If you're not serving right away, sprinkle 1 teaspoon of salt on the cucumbers after slicing them. Toss to combine and put in a colander for at least 30 minutes to remove excess water. Pat dry before mixing together the cucumber slices and yogurt mixture.

Tri-Colored Salad

Bitter radicchio and delicate endive require little in the way of preparation: Simply remove the outer leaves, chop, and add to the bowl—then relax and enjoy.

Prep & cook time | Serves 4–6

¼ **cup (60 ml) olive oil**
2 **tablespoons red wine vinegar**
Salt and ground black pepper
2 **1-inch (2.5-cm) strips of lemon peel**
2 **Belgian endives, core removed**
1 **head of radicchio, outer leaves removed**
1 **small bag of arugula**
1 **cup (225 g) shaved Parmesan cheese**

1 Whisk together the oil and vinegar. Season with salt and pepper to taste. Add the lemon peel to the mixture and let stand for 15 minutes.

2 Cut off the endive's stem, then cut into ¼-inch (5-mm) circles. Quarter the radicchio, remove the core, and cut into thin wedges.

3 Combine the arugula, endive, and radicchio in a large salad bowl.

4 Remove the lemon peel from the dressing and discard. Toss the greens with the salad dressing, scatter over the Parmesan, and adjust the seasoning, if necessary. Serve immediately.

SALADS

It's Greek to Me Salad

The secret to a good Greek salad is in the ingredients, so no skimping at the stores—make sure you buy the best.

Prep & cook time  10 min | Serves 4–6

2   **heads of romaine lettuce**
6   **ounces (175 g) cherry tomatoes**
1   **cup (115 g) pitted kalamata olives**
5   **ounces (150 g) feta, crumbled**
Juice of 1 lemon
3   **tablespoons red wine vinegar**
¼   **cup (60 ml) olive oil**
½   **tablespoon dried oregano**
Salt and ground black pepper

1. Remove the outer leaves from the romaine lettuce and discard. Separate the remaining leaves, wash, and dry. Tear the leaves into bite-size pieces and put in a bowl along with the tomatoes, olives, and feta.

2. Whisk together the lemon juice, vinegar, olive oil, and oregano. Season with salt and pepper to taste.

3. Add the dressing to the salad bowl and toss to combine. Taste for seasoning and adjust, if necessary.

4. You may want to yell out "Opa!" for good measure.

> *Swap It!*
>
> Not a big fan of tomatoes and olives? This will no longer be a Greek salad, but you can substitute 2 cups (230 g) thawed, frozen peas for the tomatoes and olives. Instead of dried oregano, use 3 tablespoons of mint, and add 4 medium sliced radishes.

Peach and Mozzarella Salad

Juicy peaches, mozzarella, and basil mingle in a sweet and savory first course that's a stunner, a cinch to make, and a crowd-pleaser—and leaves you plenty of time for fun, fun, fun.

Prep & cook time | Serves 4–6

3   **tablespoons store-bought or fresh vinaigrette salad dressing (see Fresh Dressing below)**
4   **ripe yellow or white peaches**
1   **cup (25 g) arugula**
1   **5-ounce (150-g) ball of fresh mozzarella (see page 17)**
12 **basil leaves, roughly torn**

1. Pour the vinaigrette into a bowl. Cut each peach in half and remove the pit. Quarter each half (each peach should yield eight segments) and add to the vinaigrette. Toss to coat and arrange in a single layer on a serving platter.

2. Toss the arugula in the same bowl so that it picks up any lingering vinaigrette. (The greens should be only lightly dressed so they remain crisp.) Tear the mozzarella into bite-size pieces. Tuck the cheese, arugula, and basil leaves in and around the peaches, then serve the salad immediately.

> **FRESH DRESSING**
>
> It takes just a minute to make your own salad dressing. All you need is 1 part acid (vinegar and/or lemon) mixed with 3–4 parts oil and some salt. Here's a basic recipe. Whisk 1 tablespoon of balsamic vinegar with 1 tablespoon of lemon juice, $^1/_2$ cup (60 ml) of olive oil, salt, and black pepper. Add some herbs or a teaspoon of mustard if you like.

SALADS

BLT in a Bowl

This substantial salad pays homage to the great BLT—and you won't even need the skillet. Using ripe tomatoes and good smoky bacon makes all the difference.

Prep & cook time Serves 4

- **4 slices thick-cut, smoked bacon**
- **4 medium, ripe tomatoes**
- **I ripe avocado**
- **4 cups (115 g) baby spinach, washed and dried**
- **2 tablespoons balsamic vinegar**
- **I tablespoon lemon juice**
- **¼ cup (60 ml) olive oil**
- **Salt and ground black pepper**
- **Toasted country bread, with a side of mayonnaise to serve (optional)**

❶ Line a microwave-safe plate with paper towels. Lay the bacon in a single layer on the plate and cover with another layer of paper towels. Microwave on high for 3 minutes.

❷ Turn over the bacon and microwave for another 2–3 minutes, until lightly browned and cooked to your preferred crispiness. Transfer the bacon to a clean plate, lined with fresh paper towels, and let cool.

KEEP THINGS SAFE

You will be handling raw meat, so good hygiene is important. Keep the uncooked bacon, along with any utensils used to prepare it, away from all the other ingredients—this is important because they are eaten raw. Wash your hands well after handling uncooked bacon.

28

Shop and serve!

③ Quarter the tomatoes and cut out the core. Set aside.

④ Chop up the bacon into ½-inch/1-cm pieces and set aside on a plate lined with clean paper towels.

⑤ Halve the avocado and remove the pit (use the point of a sharp kitchen knife to pry it out). Scoop out the avocado flesh with a spoon, cut into cubes, and add to a large bowl. Add the tomatoes and spinach to the bowl with the avocado.

⑥ Whisk together the vinegar, lemon juice, and olive oil. Season with salt and pepper to taste.

⑦ Pour the vinaigrette over the salad and toss to coat. Sprinkle the bacon pieces over the salad, and serve with the toast and side of mayo, if you like.

THE LITTLE LEAF THAT COULD

Baby spinach has all the health benefits of large leaf spinach. At only 7 calories a cup, it packs a healthy dose of vitamins A and C plus folate, iron, and calcium. Enjoy it, and remember "nobody puts baby spinach in the corner."

Antipasto Fantastico

To create this dinner, shop at any big supermarket, or stake out a good Italian deli. For an extra-speedy meal, serve the roasted bell peppers and artichokes straight from the jar.

Prep & cook time | Serves 4–6

1   14-ounce (400-g) jar olive oil–marinated artichokes
Juice and grated zest of 1 lemon
2   **tablespoons olive oil**
1   **16-ounce (450-g) jar roasted red bell peppers, drained and cut into strips**
½   **tablespoon balsamic vinegar**
Pinch of salt
5   **ounces (150 g) sliced prosciutto**
4   **ounces (115 g) sliced hot genoa salami**
1   **pound (450 g) fresh mozzarella (see page 17), cut into bite-size pieces**
8   **ounces (225 g) Parmesan cheese, cut into bite-size pieces**
⅔   **cup (115 g) cured black olives**
1   **slab focaccia or 1 fresh baguette, cut into ¼-inch (5-mm)-thick slices**

1 Drain the artichokes and toss with the lemon juice and zest and 1 tablespoon of olive oil in a small bowl.

2 Drain the red bell peppers and slice into strips. In a separate small bowl, toss with the remaining olive oil and the balsamic vinegar and salt.

3 Arrange the meats and cheese on a platter. Place the olives in a small bowl. Arrange the focaccia or baguette on a cutting board, then place the antipasto ingredients in the center of the table. Let your guests serve themselves.

Shop and serve!

Mean Bean and Tuna Salad

Good oil-packed tuna is more expensive, but it's well worth it. The beans stretch the tuna, so you get more for your money, and you'll have a more substantial meal on your plate.

Prep & cook time (15 min) | Serves 4–6

- **2 6-ounce (175-g) cans tuna fish, preferably packed in olive oil, drained**
- **2 15-ounce (425-g) cans cannellini or white kidney beans, drained and rinsed**
- **1 red bell pepper, cored, seeded, and cut into thin slices**
- **1 celery stalk, thinly sliced on the diagonal**
- **3 tablespoons capers, rinsed and roughly chopped**
- **1 cup (60 g) flat-leaf parsley leaves**
- **Juice and grated zest of 1 lemon**
- **1 tablespoon red wine vinegar**
- **1 tablespoon olive oil**
- **Salt and ground black pepper**
- **French bread with butter and a green salad to serve (optional)**

1. In a large bowl, combine the tuna, beans, bell pepper, celery, capers, parsley, and lemon zest.

2. Whisk together the lemon juice, vinegar, and olive oil. Season with salt and pepper to taste. Pour over the tuna-bean mixture and toss to combine.

3. Serve with french bread, butter, and a green salad, if you like.

Swap It!

Bean there, done that? Substitute the beans for a loaf of country bread, torn into pieces, to make your own *pan bagnat* salad. In France, a *pan bagnat* is a loaf of bread filled with green bell peppers, onions, tomatoes, and hard-boiled eggs, topped with a vinaigrette.

Chicken on a Raft

Make rotisserie chicken magnificent by shredding it, then mixing it with fresh ingredients. Serve it on warmed naan, and your guests will think you've been slaving away in a hot kitchen.

Prep & cook time | Serves 4–6

1½ cups (350 g) plain, whole-milk Greek yogurt
1   tablespoon lemon juice
Salt and ground black pepper
1   2-pound/900-g rotisserie chicken, skin discarded
1   teaspoon dried oregano
1   tablespoon olive oil, plus extra for brushing and drizzling
2   medium cucumbers
4   radishes, thinly sliced
1   cup (160 g) grape tomatoes, halved
½   cup (75 g) crumbled feta cheese
½   cup (25 g) chopped fresh mint,
    plus extra to garnish
4   pita breads or naan

1 In a small bowl, whisk together the yogurt and lemon juice. Season with salt and pepper to taste.

2 Pull the chicken meat from the bones and shred into bite-size pieces. Toss with the oregano, a pinch of salt, and the olive oil.

3 Cut the cucumbers in half lengthwise and slice into thin semicircles. Toss them with the radishes, tomatoes, feta, and mint. Let stand for about 10 minutes. Season with salt and pepper to taste.

4 Toast the pita or naan until lightly browned. Brush with some olive oil and season to taste with salt.

5 Spread the yogurt mixture on top of each piece of bread, distribute the chicken evenly between them, and top with the vegetable-feta mixture. Scatter with extra mint leaves to garnish and drizzle with olive oil.

> **DON'T BE BITTER!**
>
> Before slicing up the cucumber, cut off a small piece of skin to taste it. If it tastes at all bitter, peel the cucumber; if not, you can leave the skin on.

Chicken Salad with Grapes

This is my definitive chicken salad recipe. No need for a bunch of others, thank you.

Prep & cook time 15 min | Serves 4–6

1   **2-pound (900-g) rotisserie chicken**
½   **cup (115 g) mayonnaise**
Juice of ½ lemon
1   **tablespoon whole-grain Dijon mustard**
4   **celery stalks, cut into ½-inch/1-cm slices**
1   **cup (125 g) red seedless grapes**
Salt and ground black pepper
4   **pita breads or slices whole-grain bread, toasted, to serve**

1 Pull the chicken meat from the bones with your hands and discard the carcass. Cut the meat into ³/₄-inch (2-cm) pieces.

2 Put the chopped meat into a bowl and add all remaining ingredients except the bread. Toss to combine. Season with salt and pepper to taste, and serve with pita or toast.

Life's too short to chop onions

MAIN DISHES

Chicken à la Easy

Whole rotisserie chicken pieces spread out over a bed of fluffy couscous tossed with sharp arugula and red berries scattered over the top—just gorgeous!

Prep & cook time 15 min | Serves 4–6

1½ cups (350 ml) water
1   cup (175 g) instant couscous
2   cups (50 g) arugula, washed and dried
3   tablespoons sesame seeds
Juice of 1 lemon
¼   cup (60 ml) olive oil
Salt and ground black pepper
1   2-pound (900-g) rotisserie chicken
½   pint (160 g) raspberries

① Bring the water to a boil. Place the instant couscous in a deep bowl and pour the boiling water over top. Stir the mixture, cover the bowl, and let stand for about 30 seconds. Uncover and fluff up the couscous with a fork. Re-cover the bowl and let stand for 3–4 minutes. Fluff up the couscous and check that it is fully cooked (see page 37).

② Toss the couscous with the arugula, sesame seeds, lemon juice, and olive oil. Season with salt and pepper to taste.

③ Separate the chicken into whole pieces—breasts, legs, thighs, drumsticks, and wings.

④ To serve, spread out the couscous-arugula mixture on a serving platter. Arrange the chicken pieces on top, and scatter the raspberries over and around the chicken.

Shop and serve!

Instant Peanut Noodle Salad

Serve as a side dish, a vegetarian main dish, or topped with shrimp for something new. In terms of work: This version is easy, easy, easy!

Prep & cook time | Serves 4–6

1	8-ounce/225-g package **Chinese noodles**
¼	cup (60 ml) boiling water, plus extra to prepare the noodles
6	tablespoons creamy peanut butter
3	tablespoons balsamic vinegar
3	tablespoons soy sauce
1½	tablespoons sugar
1	tablespoon sesame oil
½	teaspoon cayenne pepper
2	scallions, thinly sliced on the diagonal
¼	cup (35 g) roughly chopped roasted peanuts
¼	cup (15 g) fresh cilantro leaves

1. Place the noodles in a large bowl and pour over enough boiling water to completely cover. Stir with a fork and cover with a plate for 3 minutes. Uncover and stir again to separate the noodles. Re-cover with the plate and let stand for 3 minutes, or until the noodles are al dente—that means tender but still firm. Drain and set aside.

2. In a small bowl, whisk together the ¼ cup (60 ml) of hot water and the peanut butter until smooth. Whisk in the balsamic vinegar, soy sauce, sugar, sesame oil, and cayenne pepper until well combined.

3. Toss the noodles with the dressing until evenly coated. Mix in the scallions and peanuts. Top with the cilantro leaves and serve.

Chickpea Mash

You might think that chickpeas are bland, but the garlic adds a real kick. Drizzle with extra olive oil and a sprinkle of paprika just before serving for an effortless ooh-la-la finish!

Prep & cook time   Serves 4–6

2   cloves garlic
2   15-ounce (425-g) cans chickpeas, drained and rinsed
I   teaspoon paprika, plus extra to garnish
Juice of I lemon
1½ cups (350 ml) olive oil, plus extra to garnish
Salt and ground black pepper

1 Peel the garlic and pulse in a food processor until roughly chopped. Add all the remaining ingredients and puree until smooth. Season with salt and pepper to taste.

2 Put the mixture into a microwave-safe bowl, microwave on high for I minute, and stir. Then microwave and stir the mixture at 30-second intervals until heated through.

3 To garnish, drizzle with olive oil and sprinkle with a pinch of paprika just before serving.

DO THE MASH!

In a silly mood? Why not make up a dance while you're cooking. The Monster Mash *was* once a graveyard smash, after all—you might just start the latest dance trend.

Shop and serve!

Couscous—Quick! Quick!

Serve up this delicate minute grain and you, too, will become a couscous convert in no time.

Prep & cook time **10 min**   Serves 4–6

3   cups (700 ml) water
2   cups (350 g) instant couscous
1   cup (115 g) slivered almonds
1½ cups (250 g) raisins
¼   teaspoon cinnamon
Juice of 1 orange
½   cup (120 ml) olive oil
½   cup (25 g) chopped parsley or mint
Salt and ground black pepper

❶ Bring the water to a boil. Place the couscous in a deep bowl and pour the boiling water over it. Stir the mixture, cover, and let stand for 30 seconds. Uncover and fluff up the couscous with a fork, cover again, and let stand for 3–4 minutes. Fluff up the grains again and check that the couscous is fully cooked.

❷ Add the remaining ingredients and toss to combine. Season with salt and pepper to taste and serve.

What's That?

A type of granular semolina (which is a coarsely ground durum wheat), couscous is a staple food found in many North African dishes. You'll find the instant type stacking the shelves in large supermarkets and Middle Eastern stores. This instant version is quick and easy to make (see Step 1). When fully cooked, the fluffed-up couscous grains should be soft, loose, and separate.

~ TWO ~

Slam the door and scram!

Yeah, yeah, I know I just said in Chapter One that it's OK to turn your back on your oven. But now that you sailed through the first part, I think you'll start to believe there's more to life than takeout and microwaved foods. The high heat of an oven actually makes food more flavorful, and why miss out on that? Still skeptical? The fantastic thing about roasting food is that all the work is done up front.

Yep, there's some prep time. But once that pan's in the oven, you're free. That's right. The oven does your work while you do ... nothing! Thought that would pique your interest. The bottom line is these easy-bake recipes will get you kudos for meals you barely remember making, and you'll have time for memorable moments ahead.

APPETIZERS

Roasted Mushrooms with Garlic and Parsley

Turn this rustic hors d'oeuvre into a first course and serve the warm 'shrooms alongside a green salad. It's really simple, and everyone will be impressed. Who needs smoke and mirrors?

Prep & cook time 35 min   Serves 4

- 16 medium white mushrooms, wiped clean
- 4 cloves garlic, peeled
- 2½ tablespoons olive oil
- ¾ teaspoon salt
- ½ teaspoon roughly chopped thyme leaves
- ¼ cup (35 g) dry bread crumbs
- 1 tablespoon roughly chopped fresh parsley or 1 teaspoon dried parsley

1. Preheat the oven to 400°F (200°C). Remove the stems from the mushrooms (discard or save them for another use). Slice each garlic clove into 4 slices.

2. Toss the mushrooms in a bowl with 2 tablespoons of the olive oil, ½ teaspoon of salt, and the thyme. Arrange the mushrooms on a roasting pan with their cavities facing upward. Place a garlic slice in each cavity and roast for 20 minutes, or until tender.

3. Meanwhile, place the bread crumbs, parsley, and remaining olive oil and salt in a food processor. Pulse until the mixture is fine and uniform in texture. Spread out the bread-crumb mixture in a small ovenproof dish and bake for 6 to 8 minutes, or until golden brown.

4. Arrange the mushrooms on a serving platter, sprinkle the bread-crumb mixture over the top, and serve.

Nothing-to-It Wings and Dip

Lip-smacking wings made from a few basic ingredients, and then a 1-2-3 blue cheese dip. What's not to love?

Prep & cook time | Serves 4

16 chicken wings
⅔ cup (150 ml) hot sauce
½ cup (120 ml) olive oil
1 teaspoon salt
Ground black pepper

FOR THE BLUE CHEESE DIP
8 ounces (225 g) good-quality blue cheese, such as spicy gorgonzola, roquefort, or Danish blue
⅔ cup (150 g) mayonnaise
⅔ cup (150 g) sour cream
2 teaspoons white wine vinegar
Salt and ground black pepper

❶ Toss the chicken wings with half of the hot sauce, the oil, and salt and pepper to taste. Let marinate for at least 30 minutes. Meanwhile, preheat the oven to 400°F (200°C). Lightly grease a baking sheet.

❷ Spread the wings on the greased baking sheet and roast for 55 minutes, or until tender and lightly browned. Turn the wings once or twice during roasting.

❸ Remove from the oven and place the wings in a bowl. Add the remaining hot sauce and toss well to combine. Let cool slightly, taste for seasoning, and adjust if desired.

❹ Place all the cheese dip ingredients in a food processor and pulse until combined but still chunky. Season with salt and pepper to taste, and serve with the wings.

APPETIZERS

Savory Bread Pudding

Think French onion soup in the oven—hold the stock and add the eggs. This will make you a new fan of casseroles. Thank you, oven!

Prep & cook time 1¼ hr | Serves 4

2   **tablespoons olive oil**
1   **clove garlic, smashed and peeled**
1   **white onion, sliced**
1   **tablespoon chopped fresh thyme**
½   **teaspoon salt**
2   **eggs**
¾   **cup (175 ml) milk**
½   **tablespoon butter**
4   **thick slices white bread (about 6 ounces/150 g)**
¼   **cup (30 g) grated Gruyère cheese**

1. Preheat the oven to 350°F (180°C). In a skillet, heat the olive oil over medium heat. Add the garlic to the skillet and sauté for 30 seconds.

2. Add the sliced onion, chopped thyme, and ¼ teaspoon of salt and sauté for 1 to 2 minutes. Cover the skillet and sweat the onions for about 15 minutes, or until they are completely soft and slightly golden.

3. Meanwhile, beat the eggs with the milk and the remaining salt. Using half the butter, grease an ovenproof baking dish that snugly holds the bread in a single, even layer.

4. Remove the garlic clove from the skillet. Spread the sautéed onions across the bottom of the dish and lay the bread slices on top, overlapping them slightly. Pour the egg mixture over the bread, and press down with

a spatula to make sure the bread is moistened. Scatter Gruyère over the top and dot with the remaining butter.

5 Cover the baking dish with aluminum foil and bake for 30 minutes. Remove the foil and bake for an additional 15 minutes, until the pudding is set and golden on top. Serve immediately.

Jalapeño Corn Bread

With these flourishes, no one will ever guess your corn bread was born in a box.

Prep & cook time 30 min | Serves 6

Butter or oil for greasing
1   **8½-ounce (240-g) box corn bread muffin mix**
1   **egg**
⅓   **cup (75 ml) milk**
1   **jalapeño pepper, stem removed, seeded, and thinly sliced**
¼   **cup (45 g) thawed frozen corn kernels**

1 Preheat the oven to 400°F (200°C). Grease a 6-cup muffin pan.

2 Mix together all the ingredients—the batter will be slightly lumpy. Let the batter rest for 3–5 minutes, then remix the ingredients and scoop into the muffin pan cups.

3 Bake in the preheated oven for 15–20 minutes, or until the muffins are golden brown.

Blame It on the Pretty Pork Carnitas

This faithful dish takes its time in the oven but you spend only minutes in the kitchen. A sure thing to please your guests, carnitas (the Mexican term for "little meats") is a winner.

Prep & cook time 3¾ hr   Serves 6

1   **tablespoon salt, or enough to coat the butt**
1   **2–3-pound (900-g–1.3-kg) pork butt**
2   **1-inch (2.5-cm) strips of orange peel**
3   **cloves garlic, smashed and peeled**
1   **jalapeño pepper, sliced in half**
1½ **cinnamon sticks**
2   **bay leaves**
½   **teaspoon cumin**
2   **teaspoons chili powder**
¼   **teaspoon black peppercorns**
8   **cups (2 liters) water, or enough to submerge two-thirds of the butt**

TO SERVE
1   **package corn tortillas, warmed**
1   **large ripe advocado, pitted, peeled, and sliced**
Lime wedges
2   **cups (130 g) spicy-hot salsa**
1   **cup (15 g) fresh cilantro leaves**
1½ **cups (175 g) crumbled queso fresco or other firm, mild cheese**

1 Preheat the oven to 375°F (190°C). Rub the salt all over the pork and let stand at room temperature for about 15 minutes.

Slam the door and scram!

2 Place the pork in a Dutch oven pot. Add the remaining ingredients to the pot, pour in enough water to submerge two-thirds of the meat, and cover with a lid. Roast in the oven for 3 hours. (Now is the time to sneak off.)

3 Before removing the butt from the oven, check that the meat shreds with the slightest touch. Once completely tender, transfer the pork to a cutting board. Use two forks to shred the meat.

4 If you like the meat crispy, spread it out on a baking sheet and pour 1–2 cups (240–475 ml) of the cooking liquid over it, dampening only the lower third of the meat. Roast for 15 minutes, or until the meat browns and becomes crispy. Pour off any extra liquid.

5 For a memorable taco party, serve the carnitas as the centerpiece of a spread with all the fixings: warmed corn tortillas, sliced avocado, lime wedges, salsa, cilantro, and crumbled queso fresco. (You could make your own salsa, but with the pork you'll have done enough.)

Swap It!

If you have time for lengthy braising, inexpensive pork butt is perfect, but quicker taco fillings abound. If you're in a hurry or aren't feeling porky, try one of these options. Replace the pork with shrimp (see page 111), sliced skirt steak (see page 85), roasted vegetables (see page 66), or herb-y halibut (see page 90, but hold the seasonings and lemons). Or you can sauté a can of drained and rinsed black beans with a little oil, cumin, salt, and black pepper. If your stove allergy is really acting up, forget about cooking altogether and shred up a store-bought rotisserie chicken (see pages 32–33).

Chicken Breasts with Beans and Tomatoes

Keep the takeout menus in your drawer—here's a one-dish dinner perfect for weeknight suppers.

Prep & cook time 1¼ hr | Serves 4

6   sprigs rosemary
4   bone-in chicken breasts, washed and patted dry
Salt and ground black pepper
2   15-ounce (425-g) cans cannellini or northern beans, drained, rinsed, and dried
⅓   cup (75 ml) olive oil, plus extra for drizzling
½   teaspoon dried red pepper flakes
I   12-ounce (350-g) container cherry tomatoes, halved
½   cup (120 ml) white wine
8   cloves garlic, smashed, peeled, and chopped

❶ Preheat the oven to 450°F (230°C). Position a rack in the center of the oven. Break the rosemary sprigs in half.

❷ Season both sides of the chicken with salt and pepper. Press half a rosemary sprig into each side. Arrange the chicken, skin side up, in a large casserole dish.

❸ Toss the beans with the remaining herb sprigs and all the remaining ingredients. Season the beans with salt and pepper. Scatter the bean-tomato mixture around the chicken. Drizzle with extra olive oil.

❹ Transfer the dish to the oven and bake for 50 minutes, or until the chicken is cooked through. Remove the rosemary sprigs and serve.

Slam the door and scram!

Chicken Legs with Wine and Olives

What makes this dish so great? The wine? The olives? The thyme? They help, but no—there's just no chopping.

Prep & cook time 1¼ hr | Serves 4

4	**chicken legs, skin on**
3	**tablespoons olive oil**
6	**sprigs of thyme or 1½ teaspoons dried thyme**
½	**tablespoon salt**
½	**teaspoon red pepper flakes**
10	**garlic cloves, gently smashed and peeled**
1	**cup (240 ml) white wine**
16	**olives, green or black, pitted or whole**

① Preheat the oven to 450°F (230°C). Position a rack in the center of the oven. Toss the chicken with the oil, thyme, salt, and pepper flakes. Rub the seasonings into the meat.

② Arrange the chicken, skin side up, in a large ovenproof dish. Scatter the garlic over the chicken and roast for 20 minutes, or until the skin begins to brown.

③ Add the wine and olives, and roast in the oven for 25–35 minutes, until cooked through. Let the chicken stand for about 10 minutes before serving.

> ### Swap It!
> If you don't mind a bit of chopping, cut 3 slices of thick bacon into 1-inch (2.5-cm) pieces and 1 large red onion into 8 wedges. Scatter these with the garlic over and around the chicken legs in Step 3, and omit the olives. Proceed as directed.

Life's too short to chop onions

MAIN DISHES

Roasted Chicken, Four Ways

You don't need to be a chicken about making roast chicken. Why? Well … because there's really nothing to it.

Prep & cook time 1¾ hr | Serves 4

I	**4-pound (1.8-kg) chicken**
2	**teaspoons salt**
½	**teaspoon black pepper**
2	**tablespoons olive oil**
I	**cup (240 ml) wine or water**

1 Preheat the oven to 450°F (230°C). Position a rack in the lower third of the oven. Pat the chicken dry, season the outside with half the salt and pepper, and rub the oil over the skin. Toss the remaining salt and pepper into the cavity.

2 Place the chicken, breast side up, in a roasting pan. Roast for 20 minutes, until the breast is firm and browned in spots. Add ½ cup (120 ml) wine to the pan. Turn the chicken breast side down. Reduce the oven temperature to 375°F (190°C) and roast for 30 minutes, until browned.

3 Turn the chicken breast side up. Roast for 30 minutes, until cooked and the juices run clear when pierced in the thickest part with a skewer, or a meat thermometer, inserted into the inner thigh, reads 180°F (82°C).

4 Transfer to a cutting board and let rest for 10 minutes before carving. To serve the chicken with the pan juices, tilt the chicken to drain its cavity juices into the pan. Spoon off the fat, set the pan over a high heat, and add the remaining wine; scrape up any brown sediment as you stir. Strain the pan sauce and serve with the roasted chicken.

Slam the door and scram!

VARIATIONS

LEMON CHICKEN

Remove the zest (the colored part of the rind) from 2 lemons using a grater, and squeeze out their juices. Rub the zest and juice over the skin of the chicken with the oil in Step 1. Cut up 2 lemons and add them to the cavity, along with a halved bulb of garlic. Cover the chicken, marinate in the refrigerator for at least 2 hours, then roast as directed.

CHICKEN WITH GARLIC AND HERBS

Before Step 2, pulse together 3 tablespoons softened, unsalted butter, a tablespoon each of rosemary and thyme, a sage leaf, and the zest of 1 lemon in a food processor. Season with salt and pepper. Using your fingers, separate the skin from the breast meat. Rub half the herb butter under the skin and half over the chicken. Put a halved bulb of garlic and lemon into the cavity with 2 sprigs each of thyme and rosemary and 2 sage leaves. Proceed as directed.

ADD A BREAD SALAD

A bread salad soaks up chicken juices beautifully. Cut a 1-pound (450-g) loaf of sourdough bread into cubes, and spread them in a roasting pan. Prepare the chicken as described in Step 1. Place a roasting rack into the pan and the chicken on top, and roast as directed. When the chicken is done, transfer it to a cutting board. Put the bread cubes in a large bowl and toss with 2 cored tomatoes cut into 1-inch (2.5-cm) wedges, 1/4 cup (60 ml) olive oil, the juice of 1 lemon, 1/2 cup (25 g) roughly chopped parsley, and any pan juice. Season with salt and pepper to taste. Serve warm with the chicken.

Bacon Meatloaf

This Sunday standby is a breeze. Use leftovers in sandwiches for Meatloaf Monday, and you'll have two days where you're barely in the kitchen.

Prep & cook time 1½ hr | Serves 4–6

I   **medium onion, quartered**
I   **medium carrot, cut into 1-inch (2.5-cm) pieces**
2   **cloves garlic, smashed and peeled**
I   **teaspoon thyme**
½   **cup (120 g) ketchup**
I   **tablespoon tomato paste**
2   **tablespoons Worcestershire sauce**
1½   **cups (210 g) dry bread crumbs or 3 slices stale white bread, pulsed until crumbly**
2   **large eggs**
1½   **pounds (675 g) ground beef**
3   **thick slices bacon**

❶ Preheat the oven to 375°F (190°C).

❷ In a food processor, pulse the onion, carrot, garlic, and thyme together until medium fine. In a mixing bowl, mix together the pulsed vegetables with the remaining ingredients, except the bacon, until just combined.

❸ Transfer the meat to a medium-small loaf pan. Lay the bacon slices over the top, overlapping them slightly.

❹ Roast in the preheated oven for 1 hour, or until the bacon is crispy and the meat is cooked through. Strain off the excess fat by tilting the loaf pan up and over. Serve warm.

Baked Chicken Meatballs

Browning meatballs in a hot pan is a thing of the past. If you've never tried your luck before, now you'll never have to.

Prep & cook time 1 hr | Serves 4–6

Olive oil for greasing
½ **yellow onion**
3 **cloves garlic, smashed and peeled**
2 **slices day-old white bread, crusts removed and torn**
1 **large egg**
¼ **cup (60 ml) milk**
½ **cup (25 g) loosely packed parsley**
2 **tablespoons olive oil**
1½ **teaspoons dried oregano**
1½ **teaspoons salt**
1 **teaspoon freshly ground pepper**
½ **cup freshly grated Parmesan cheese**
1½ **pounds (675 g) ground chicken**

1 Preheat the oven to 375°F (190°C). Brush a baking sheet with oil. Put all the ingredients except the chicken in a food processor and pulse until fine. Put the chicken in a bowl, add the processed ingredients, and stir to combine.

2 Form the mixture into golf-ball-size balls and place them on the baking sheet ½-inch (1-cm) apart. Bake in the oven for 30–40 minutes, until browned and cooked through.

HAVE A BALL
Broil the meatballs smothered with tomato sauce (see page 76) and serve with pasta. Other ideas? Serve with a warm potato salad, or toss them into a vegetable bean soup.

51

MAIN DISHES

Ribs Extra

These Asian-inspired ribs are extra flavorful. All you do is toss, marinate, and roast. You can handle that, right?

Prep & cook time, plus marinating 1¾ hr | Serves 4–6 |◯|

¼ **cup (60 ml) soy sauce**
2 **teaspoons whole cardamom seeds**
3 **whole stars of anise**
I **teaspoon allspice berries**
¼ **teaspoon cayenne**
4 **cloves garlic, smashed and roughly chopped**
6 **tablespoons honey**
2½ **pounds (1.2 kg) pork ribs**

1 Place all the ingredients in a roasting pan and toss to combine. Let the ribs marinate, covered, in the refrigerator, for at least I hour or overnight.

2 Preheat the oven to 350°F (180°C).

3 Roast the ribs for I hour 20 minutes, or until cooked through. Turn the meat once or twice during roasting. Let the ribs stand for about 10 minutes before serving.

> **BBQ TIME!**
> Kick off the BBQ season with these ribs and traditional corn on the cob or baked beans. Or be more creative and serve them with Peach and Mozzarella Salad (see page 27), Jalapeño Corn Bread (see page 43), or Unforgettable Mac and Cheese (see page 56).

Slam the door and scram!

Lamb Skewers

Kebabs are a snap: Just ask your butcher to cube the meat while you daydream at the counter …

Prep & cook time, plus marinating **40 min** | Serves 4–6

1½ **pounds (675 g) lamb sirloin, cut into 1½-inch (4-cm) cubes**
2 **tablespoons freshly chopped rosemary or 2 teaspoons dried rosemary**
2 **teaspoons ground black pepper**
2 **tablespoons soy sauce**
¼ **teaspoon cumin**
Grated zest and juice of 1 lemon
2 **cloves garlic, peeled and smashed**
Oil for greasing

1 Presoak 8–12 wooden skewers in water for 30 minutes.

2 Meanwhile, combine all the ingredients except the oil in a bowl, cover, and refrigerate for at least 15 minutes. Marinating the lamb for 4 hours or overnight imparts a lot of flavor, so if you plan ahead, you'll be rewarded.

3 Preheat the oven to 375°F (190°C) and lightly grease a baking sheet. Bring the lamb to room temperature. Discard the garlic and thread 3–4 pieces of lamb onto each skewer, leaving room between each piece. For even cooking, skewer pieces of the same size together.

4 Spread the skewers out on the baking sheet. Bake, turning them once or twice during cooking, to the desired doneness; 8–10 minutes for medium rare. Serve with couscous (page 37) or warm pita bread, if you want.

MAIN DISHES

Salmon Two Ways

Salmon requires little in the way of real work. You can serve it plain—or add a topping to transform your broiled salmon into something that will impress everyone.

Prep & cook time 45 min | Serves 4

1½ **pounds (675 g) center cut wild salmon, cut into 4 fillets**
2 **teaspoons salt**
½ **teaspoon ground black pepper**
1 **tablespoon olive oil, plus extra for greasing**

1 Preheat the oven to 400°F (200°C). Line a baking sheet with parchment paper and lightly oil the parchment.

2 Season both sides of the salmon with salt and pepper. Rub in the olive oil. Place the salmon on the baking sheet, skin side down. Bake for 15 to 20 minutes, until the salmon is just cooked through and flakes easily. Remove from the oven and let stand 10 minutes before serving.

VARIATION

SALMON WITH A HERB TOPPING

To serve with an herb topping, pulse 1 shallot in a food processor until finely chopped. Add ¼ cup (10 g) each of fresh parsley and dill and the zest of 1 lemon. Pulse until finely chopped. Place the mixture in a small bowl and stir in 2 tablespoons of olive oil. Season with salt and pepper to taste. Coat the top of the fish with the herb mixture before placing in the oven in Step 2.

Black Cod with Olive Relish

Want to eat more protein-packed fish, but don't know how to cook it? Good news: Fish is quick to make and easy to dress up.

Prep & cook time | Serves 4

4 cod fillets, about 1¼-inch (3-cm) thick (1½ pounds/675 g in total weight)
¾ teaspoon salt
¼ teaspoon ground black pepper
2 tablespoons olive oil

FOR THE OLIVE RELISH
¾ cup (85 g) pitted green olives, drained and rinsed
2 tablespoons chopped fresh parsley
Grated zest of 1 lemon
¼ cup (60 ml) olive oil
1 teaspoon lemon juice
Salt and ground black pepper

❶ Preheat the oven to 400°F (200°C). Season both sides of the cod with salt and pepper and rub in the olive oil. Place them on a baking sheet and cook for about 10–12 minutes, until it flakes apart easily and is just white.

❷ Place the olives, parsley, and lemon zest into a food processor and pulse until coarsely chopped and uniform. Transfer to a bowl and stir in the olive oil and lemon juice. Season with salt and pepper to taste. Serve the fish with the relish.

> **SPOILED FOR CHOICE**
> If you are running out of time, skip the olive relish and serve the cod plain with a drizzle of olive oil and lemon wedges on the side. Not shabby in the least.

Unforgettable Mac and Cheese

Thankfully, this version is streamlined and, frankly, incomparably delicious. This is your go-to mac and cheese.

Prep & cook time I hr | Serves 4–6

- I **pound (450 g) medium shells, rigatoni, or penne**
- I **tablespoon olive oil**
- I **cup (240 ml) heavy cream**
- ¾ **cup (175 ml) whole milk**
- I **large egg, lightly beaten**
- ½ **teaspoon nutmeg**
- ½ **teaspoon salt**
- ¼ **teaspoon ground black pepper**
- **Pinch of cayenne pepper**
- 2 **ounces (50 g) cream cheese, room temperature**
- I **pound (450 g) sharp cheddar cheese, grated**
- ¼ **cup (15 g) crushed cheese crackers**
- I **tablespoon butter, cut into pieces, plus extra for greasing**

1 Preheat the oven to 350°F (180°C). Butter a large ovenproof dish. Bring a pot of salted water to a rolling boil. Add the pasta and cook for 8–10 minutes, until just al dente, or follow the directions on the package. Drain and toss the pasta with the olive oil.

2 Meanwhile, whisk together the cream, milk, egg, nutmeg, salt, pepper, and cayenne.

3 Reserve ¼ cup (30 g) of the cheddar cheese for the topping. In a large bowl, toss the pasta shells with the milk mixture, the cream cheese, and the remaining cheddar cheese.

④ Scrape the mac and cheese into the prepared dish and bake on the middle rack for 20 minutes. Remove the dish from the oven and top with the reserved cheese and crushed crackers, and dot with the butter. Return the dish to the oven, placing it on the top rack, and bake an additional 15 minutes, until lightly browned.

> **HAM IT UP!**
> For a ham-y version, add 8 ounces (225 g) thickly sliced, good-quality deli ham cut into cubes with the cheese and shells in Step 3. Then bake as directed.

Molasses Baked Beans

This is a great side dish made mostly from pantry ingredients. Here's to one less trip to the supermarket.

Prep & cook time Serves 4–6

- **8   ounces (225 g) thick bacon cut into ¼-inch (5-mm) pieces**
- **1   large onion, sliced**
- **2   15-ounce (425-g) can of pinto beans, drained and rinsed**
- **¼   cup (50 g) brown sugar**
- **¼   cup (100 g) molasses**
- **¼   teaspoon cayenne pepper**
- **¼   teaspoon salt**

Preheat the oven to 350°F (180°C). Heat a sauté pan over medium heat, add the bacon, and cook for 4 minutes, until it browns. Add the onion and fry for 5 minutes, until soft. Add the remaining ingredients; simmer for 5 minutes, until the sugar melts. Put in a baking dish, cover, and bake for 30 minutes.

SIDE DISHES

One Potato, Two Potato Gratin

Potato gratins are hard to resist. Here's a version that will provide tons of nutrients and look fantastic on your table.

Prep & cook time 1 hr | Serves 4

I   **clove garlic, halved**
I   **tablespoon melted butter**
2   **medium Yukon gold potatoes, peeled**
I   **medium sweet potato, peeled**
Salt and ground black pepper
½   **teaspoon fresh thyme**
¼   **teaspoon nutmeg**
I   **cup grated Gruyère cheese**
I   **cup (240 ml) heavy cream**
½   **tablespoon butter**

1 Preheat the oven to 400°F (200°C). Rub a large baking dish with the cut side of the garlic and brush with the melted butter.

2 Slice both the gold and sweet potatoes ¼-inch (5-mm) thick. Switching between the potato types, arrange a layer on the bottom of the baking dish. Season with salt, pepper, thyme, and nutmeg—

Swap It!

This recipe is easy to adjust. Omit the spinach or use only one type of potato. Leave out the thyme, nutmeg, or both. Swap the cheese for another or none, whatever you fancy. Use chicken broth, olive oil, milk, or a combination instead of cream. Or, just let a good thing be.

don't use all at once, so you can season each layer. Repeat until half the potatoes have been used. Place half the Gruyère evenly over the potatoes.

3 Continue layering the potatoes and seasoning as before until all the potatoes are stacked. Pour the cream over the top—it should cover three-quarters of the gratin. Top with more cream if needed. Push down on the potatoes with a spatula.

4 Top with the remaining cheese and dot with the butter. Bake in the preheated oven for 45 minutes, until the top is brown and the potatoes are easily pierced with a knife.

Baked Ricotta

A surprising side that tastes of the best part of white pizza— the cheese.

Prep & cook time | Serves 4–6

3   pounds (1.3 kg) whole milk ricotta
6   tablespoons olive oil
½ tablespoon chopped fresh thyme
Pinch of cayenne
Salt and ground black pepper

Preheat the oven to 450°F (238°C). Place all the ingredients in a bowl and mix together well. Season with salt and pepper to taste. Spoon the mixture into a medium ovenproof dish and spread it out evenly. Bake for about 40 minutes, until the center is just firm and the bubbling top golden brown.

Cauliflower Gratin

*Fennel seeds will add character to roasted cauliflower.
Doesn't that sound intriguing?*

Prep & cook time 1 hr | Serves 4

1   head of cauliflower
2   tablespoons olive oil
1   tablespoon fennel seeds
¼   **cup (60 ml) white wine**
Salt and ground black pepper
½   **cup (40 g) grated Parmesan cheese**

① Preheat the oven 450°F (230°C). Remove the outer
leaves around the cauliflower and separate into equal-
size florets. In an ovenproof dish large enough to hold
the florets in a single layer, toss the cauliflower with the
olive oil, fennel seeds, and wine. Season with salt and
pepper to taste.

② Roast on the top rack for 30 minutes, turning once
during the cooking time. Top with the cheese and bake
for another 15 minutes, or until the cauliflower is lightly
browned and easily pierced with a knife.

Brazen Broccoli

Broccoli in the oven? Why not?

Prep & cook time 40 min | Serves 4

1	**large head of broccoli, broken into florets**
2	**tablespoons olive oil**
¼	**teaspoon salt**
7	**cloves garlic, smashed and peeled**
½	**teaspoon red pepper flakes**

Juice and grated zest of ½ lemon

Preheat the oven to 400°F (200°C). Toss together the broccoli, oil, salt, garlic, and pepper flakes in a baking dish. Bake for 20 minutes, or until easily pierced with a knife. Toss with the lemon zest and juice before serving.

Roasted Sweet Potato Fries

Here's a diet-friendly fry, skipping the stove-top altogether, that won't leave you missing the original.

Prep & cook time 35 min | Serves 4

2	**sweet potatoes, peeled and cut into 1-inch wedges**
2	**tablespoons olive oil**
½	**teaspoon salt**

Preheat the oven to 400°F (200°C). Toss together all the ingredients and roast in the oven for 20 minutes, turning after 10 minutes, until cooked through.

SIDE DISHES

Roasted Butternut Mash

To guarantee holiday cheer, make the adults happy by adding 2 tablespoons maple syrup and 1½ tablespoons bourbon to the mash.

Prep & cook time 1½ hr | Serves 4–6

1	**2–3 pound (900 k–1.3 kg) butternut squash**
2	**tablespoons olive oil**
¼	**teaspoon salt**
2	**tablespoons butter**
1	**tablespoon maple syrup**

Salt and ground black pepper

1 Preheat the oven to 400°F (200°C). Line a roasting pan with aluminum foil.

2 Halve the squash lengthwise and scoop out the seeds. Drizzle the flesh with the olive oil and sprinkle with the salt. Roast, cut side down, for 40–60 minutes, or until the squash is easily pierced with the tip of a knife. Remove from the oven.

3 When the squash is cool enough to handle, scoop the flesh into a medium bowl. Mash until smooth and uniform in texture. Stir in the butter and maple syrup. Season with salt and pepper to taste.

LEFTOVERS?

What can you do with leftover puree? Spread it out in a casserole dish and brush with oil. Bake until the top is crusty and firm. Or, smear some on a savory pie crust for tasty hors d'oeuvres or a memorable tart.

Bacon-Flecked Sprouts

In this case, bacon and Brussels sprouts make a fantastic couple. Not a fan of sprouts? Try fresh sprouts and turn over a new leaf.

Prep & cook time | Serves 4

1	**pound (450 g) Brussels sprouts**
8	**ounces (225 g) bacon, sliced crosswise**
2	**tablespoons olive oil**
¼	**teaspoon salt**
¼	**teaspoon ground black pepper**
1	**teaspoon fresh thyme**

1 Preheat the oven to 400°F (200°C). Bring a pot of salted water to a boil.

2 Meanwhile, using a sharp knife, remove the sprout ends. Trimming the ends should make the outer, damaged leaves fall off; if not, remove them. Rinse under cold running water.

3 Add the sprouts to the boiling water and cook for about 5 minutes. Drain and, when cool enough to handle, slice them in half.

4 Toss with the remaining ingredients and transfer to an ovenproof dish. Bake for 30 minutes, or until the bacon is crispy and the sprouts are nicely browned.

SIDE DISHES

Any-Thyme Tomatoes

As all good things should be, this side dish is accommodating and undemanding. Serve at room temperature or warm, with fish, meat, or poultry, broiled, roasted, or sautéed.

Prep & cook time 45 min   Serves 4

3 **tablespoons olive oil**
1½–2 pounds (675–900 g) tomatoes, cored and cut into 1½-inch (4-cm) wedges
1 **bulb of garlic, broken into whole cloves**
1½ tablespoons fresh thyme, roughly chopped, or ¾ tablespoon herbes de Provence
¼ **teaspoon salt**
¼ **teaspoon ground black pepper**

1 Preheat the oven to 375°F (190°C). Grease an ovenproof dish with 1 tablespoon of the oil.

2 Put the tomatoes, cut side up, in the prepared dish. Distribute the garlic cloves around them. Sprinkle the thyme, salt, and pepper over the top. Evenly drizzle the remaining olive oil over the tomatoes.

3 Roast in the preheated oven for about 30 minutes, until the tomatoes are lightly charred on the outside.

Swap It!
There is a perfectly good no-chop alternative to using normal tomatoes. Use cherry tomatoes in Step 2, but roast the dish at 400°F (200°C) for about 10 minutes, or until the skins just begin to split open. For a dramatic look, buy cherry tomatoes on the vine. Clip into individual portions and proceed as described above.

Roasted Asparagus, Plain and Simple

Don't sweat it if the lemon and Parmesan aren't on hand.
Roasted asparagus is good enough to stand alone.

Prep & cook time | Serves 4

1–1½ pounds (450–675 g) asparagus spears, trimmed of
    the woody ends about 1 inch (2.5 cm) from the base
1½   tablespoons olive oil
Salt and ground black pepper
¼   cup (20 g) grated Parmesan cheese
Juice and grated zest of 1 lemon

1 Preheat the broiler. Spread the asparagus out in an even
layer on a baking sheet. Drizzle with the olive oil, season
with salt and pepper, and toss to coat. Broil for 6 minutes
and turn over with tongs. Broil for another 6 minutes, or
until crisp-tender and beginning to brown.

2 Remove the asparagus from the broiler, toss with the
Parmesan and lemon zest and juice, and serve.

VARIATION

ASPARAGUS WITH MUSTARD SAUCE

Serve the spears with this quick stand-in for hollandaise,
without cracking an egg. Whisk together 1 teaspoon of
mustard, ⅓ cup (75 g) of crème fraîche (see page 21) or
mayo, and the juice of ½ lemon. Season with salt and
pepper to taste. Serve the dip alongside or over the top
of roasted asparagus.

SIDE DISHES

Springtime Roasted Veggies

What better time to serve this vegetable medley than when asparagus is at its peak. And this dish doesn't take much work, so you'll have more spring in your step later on.

Prep & cook time 50 min | Serves 4

1   **pound (450 g) small new potatoes, scrubbed and cut into quarters**
1   **teaspoon salt**
2   **tablespoons olive oil**
1   **pound (450 g) asparagus spears, trimmed of the woody ends about 1 inch (2.5 cm) from the base**
1   **bulb fennel, outer layers removed, cut into 1-inch (2.5-cm) wedges**
¼   **teaspoon pepper**
¼   **cup (12.5 g) roughly chopped or torn basil**
Juice and grated zest of 1 lemon

1 Preheat oven to 425°F (220°C). On a large baking sheet, toss the potatoes with ½ teaspoon of the salt and 1 tablespoon of the olive oil. Roast for 20 minutes.

2 Toss the asparagus and fennel with the remaining olive oil and salt and with the pepper.

3 Remove the baking sheet from the oven and add the asparagus and fennel. Use a metal spatula to toss and turn the vegetables together to coat them in the oil.

4 Return the sheet to the oven and roast for 15 minutes, or until all the vegetables are tender and easily pierced with a sharp knife. Transfer the vegetables to a serving platter and sprinkle the basil and lemon zest and juice on top.

Winter-Warming Veggies

A versatile medley that's perfect for the cooler months of the year, when parsnips are at their best.

Prep & cook time 45 min | Serves 4

I   **pound (450 g) parsnips, cut into 1½-inch (4-cm) pieces**
I   **pound (450 g) carrots, cut into 1½-inch (4-cm) pieces**
10 **garlic cloves, peeled**
I   **red onion, cut into 1½-inch (4-cm) wedges**
I   **teaspoon fresh thyme**
2   **tablespoons olive oil**
½   **teaspoon salt**
¼   **teaspoon ground black pepper**

1 Preheat the oven to 425°F (220°C). On a large baking sheet, toss the vegetables with the thyme, olive oil, salt, and pepper, then spread them into a single layer.

2 Bake in the oven for 15 minutes. Turn the vegetables with a metal spatula. Roast an additional 10–15 minutes, or until all the vegetables are tender.

TIME TO VEG

Roasted veggies served with couscous (see page 37) and a yogurt dressing will make a substantial, meat-free meal, or serve them with sautéed spinach and a bean puree, such as the Chickpea Mash (see page 36).

THREE

One pan?
Thank you, ma'am!

Who says you need to mess up a whole bunch of pots
and pans just to get one meal on the table? With these
recipes, you only need one. That's right, just one! If you
absolutely hate doing dishes, you'll love the stove-top,
one-pot wonders in this chapter. Feeding a hungry family,
hosting a lunch, or entertaining out-of-town guests? Here's
your one-pot solution. Some are classics, such as lentil
soup or chili. Others (such as my salade Niçoise) could
easily dirty three pots along the way, but they don't.

My goal is to show you how to make fabulous food
without hard work. There's no better way than with
these delicious one-pot recipes. So let the other pots
get jealous. You've met "The One."

Grilled Cheese Sticks

Turn the food of childhood memories into hors d'oeuvres for adults. To ensure the best oozing cheese, grate the cheese and cover the pan.

Prep & cook time 10 min | Serves 4

- **2   tablespoons butter, softened**
- **4   slices white sandwich bread, about ½-inch (1-cm) thick**
- **⅔   cup (75 g) grated sharp cheddar cheese**

1 Spread butter on one side of each bread slice.

2 Lay 2 slices of bread, buttered side down, on a clean surface. Distribute the cheese evenly between these 2 slices. Top with the remaining slices of bread, buttered side up.

3 Heat a nonstick pan over medium-low heat for about 1–2 minutes. Place the sandwiches in the pan and cover with a lid. Cook for about 2 minutes, or until the bottom is golden brown and the cheese is melted.

4 Flip over the sandwiches and press down with a spatula. Cook, uncovered, for another 2 minutes, or until the bread is golden and crispy.

5 Slice the sandwiches into 1-inch (2.5-cm) sticks and pass around during cocktail hour. Or have a beer and eat an unsliced grilled cheese sandwich for a quick meal.

> *Swap It!*
> I sometimes use ciabatta bread, rye, or wheat instead of white bread, and swap the cheddar for Monterey Jack, Swiss, provolone, or a fancy taleggio. It's easy to embellish, too: Add diced apples, ham, or arugula.

No-Flip Omelet

Omelets are so easy. It helps that my version eliminates the need to flip. You won't have egg on your shoes—or on your face.

Prep & cook time | Serves 8 (4 as main meal)

- **6 large eggs**
- **¼ teaspoon salt**
- **Pinch of ground black pepper**
- **1½ tablespoons butter**
- **1½ tablespoons chopped fresh herbs or 1½ teaspoons dried herbs (thyme, parsley, and/or chives)**
- **4 ounces (115 g) fresh goat cheese, crumbled**

1 Whisk together the eggs, salt, and pepper in a bowl.

2 Heat a medium sauté pan over medium-high heat for 30–60 seconds. Swirl in the butter. When melted, add the eggs and swirl around the pan. As the eggs start to set, use a spatula to pull the cooked edges toward the center and tilt the pan to move the uncooked eggs toward the perimeter. After 1–2 minutes, when the eggs appear half cooked along the edges and bottom, place a lid over the pan. Cook for 30–60 seconds, or until the center is just set.

3 Remove the lid; run a spatula around the omelet to loosen it from the pan. Turn off the heat. Transfer to a plate and sprinkle with the herbs and cheese.

HIP TO FLIP?

To serve the omelet on a platter, I hold the pan with one hand (in an oven mitt) and the plate upside down over the pan with the other hand. Holding the two firmly together, I turn everything over so the omelet falls out of the pan and onto the plate.

The Ultimate Lentil Soup

Wholesome and delicious, earthy lentil soup is a satisfying one-pot meal. What more can a legume offer?

Prep & cook time 1¾ hr   Serves 8

¼   **cup (60 ml) olive oil**
3   **tablespoons tomato paste**
3   **large leeks, white and tender green portions only, halved lengthwise, sliced ¼-inch (5-mm) thick, soaked, washed, and drained in a colander**
2   **large carrots, halved and cut into ¼-inch (5-mm) semicircles**
1½ **teaspoons cumin**
1   **tablespoon fresh thyme**
1   **cup (190 g) lentils, rinsed and drained**
6   **cups (1.4 L) chicken stock or water**
1   **bulb garlic, halved**
2   **bay leaves**
1   **cup (240 ml) red wine**
Salt and ground black pepper
Parmesan cheese to garnish (optional)

1 In a stock pot set over medium heat, heat the olive oil. Add the tomato paste, leeks, carrots, cumin, and thyme. Sauté for 10 minutes, or until the onions and vegetables are soft.

2 Add the lentils, chicken stock, garlic, and bay leaves. Bring to a boil and simmer for 1 hour.

3 Add the wine and simmer for 20 minutes to burn off the alcohol. Discard the garlic and bay leaves. Season with salt and pepper to taste.

4 Serve the soup with Parmesan grated over the top.

One pan? Thank you, ma'am!

Classic Potato Leek Soup

My favorite version of potato leek soup also happens to be one of the easiest. Velvety and sumptuous, this recipe is a winner.

Prep & cook time (1 hr) | Serves 6

1   **tablespoon olive oil**
2   **tablespoons butter**
3   **large leeks, white and tender green portions only, halved lengthwise, sliced ¼-inch (5-mm) thick, soaked, washed, and drained in a colander**
¼   **teaspoon salt, plus extra for seasoning**
1   **pound (450 g) russet potatoes, cut into ½-inch (1-cm) cubes**
8½ cups (2 L) whole milk
⅛   **teaspoon ground nutmeg**
Ground black pepper
½   **cup (120 ml) heavy cream**

1 In a stockpot set over medium heat, heat the olive oil and butter until melted. Add the leeks and stir in the salt. Reduce the heat to low and sweat the leeks (this means cooking them covered, over low heat) for about 3 minutes, until soft and limp but not browned.

2 Add the potatoes, 8 cups (1.9 L) of the milk, and the nutmeg. Simmer gently (do not boil) for 30 minutes, or until the potatoes are tender, stirring from time to time.

3 Puree the soup in a food processor, if necessary in two or three batches, until smooth.

4 Return the soup to the pot and stir in the cream and the remaining milk. Season with salt and pepper to taste. Bring back to a simmer and cook for 1 to 2 minutes. The soup thickens as it cools, so serve it piping hot.

Red Rice Royale

If searching for that must-have bag left you without time for grocery shopping, raid your pantry to make this Mediterranean-inspired recipe.

Prep & cook time 45 min | Serves 4–6

3   **tablespoons olive oil**
1   **onion, thinly sliced**
1   **green bell pepper, cored, seeded, and cubed**
1   **red bell pepper, cored, seeded, and cubed**
3   **cloves garlic, peeled and coarsely chopped**
2   **tablespoons tomato paste**
½   **teaspoon paprika**
1   **28-ounce (800-g) can crushed tomatoes**
2   **cups (475 ml) chicken or vegetable stock or water**
Salt and ground black pepper
1   **cup (200 g) white short-grain rice**

1 In a stockpot set over medium-high heat, heat the oil. Add the onion, bell peppers, garlic, tomato paste, and paprika. Sauté for about 10 minutes, or until the vegetables are soft.

2 Add the crushed tomatoes, stock or water, salt, and ground pepper. Bring to a boil and add the rice. Reduce the heat to medium low and simmer for 15–20 minutes, or until the rice is tender. Season to taste, and serve.

One pan? Thank you, ma'am!

Niçoise: Tout Simples

My streamlined version of salade Niçoise will take you to the sunny shores of the Riviera—without the price of a plane ticket!

Prep & cook time  45 min | Serves 4–6

1   **pound (450 g) green beans, trimmed**
2   **ripe medium tomatoes, cut into 2-inch (5-cm) wedges**
¾   **cup (130 g) Niçoise olives, with or without pits**
1½ **cups (350 ml) store-bought or fresh (see page 27) salad dressing**
8   **small red potatoes, scrubbed**
4   **large eggs**
1½ **cups (90 g) roughly chopped or pulsed parsley**
Salt and ground black pepper
Lemon juice to taste
1   **10-ounce (275-g) can oil-packed tuna, drained and flaked**

1 Bring a large pot of water to a boil, add the beans, and cook for 3 minutes. Transfer the beans with a slotted spoon to drain in a colander. Place the beans, tomatoes, and olives in a large bowl. Toss with half of the salad dressing.

2 Meanwhile, add the potatoes to the boiling water and cook for 15 minutes, until easily pierced with the tip of a knife. Transfer to a colander to dry. Add the eggs to the boiling water and simmer for 9–10 minutes, then transfer to a colander and cool under running water.

3 Quarter the potatoes and add to the beans. Toss with the parsley and 2–3 tablespoons of the dressing. Season with salt, pepper, and lemon juice to taste.

4 Peel and halve the eggs. Arrange the tossed vegetables, eggs, and tuna on a platter. Season with salt, lemon juice, and the remaining dressing and serve.

Painless Penne

*Save your money and forget about the jarred tomato sauce.
This sauce is ready in only 8 minutes—it's easy to make while
you wait for the pasta water to boil.*

Prep & cook time | Serves 4–6

- 1 **pound (450 g) penne pasta**
- 1/4 **cup (60 ml) olive oil, plus extra for tossing with the pasta**
- 1/2 **teaspoon crushed red pepper flakes**
- 1/2 **teaspoon salt**
- 3 **medium garlic cloves, smashed and peeled**
- 1 **28-ounce (800-g) can crushed tomatoes**
- 1/2 **teaspoon sugar**
- **Ground black pepper**
- 8 **basil leaves, torn**
- 1/4 **cup (30 g) cubed, fresh mozzarella cheese**

1. Bring a pot of salted water to a boil. Add the penne and boil for 8 minutes, until al dente, or cook according to the package directions. Reserve 1/2 cup (120 ml) of the cooking liquid and set aside. Drain the pasta and toss with just enough extra olive oil to keep it from sticking.

2. Meanwhile, place the olive oil, red pepper flakes, salt, and garlic in a large sauté pan. Place the pan over medium heat and cook for 1–2 minutes, until fragrant. Stir in the tomatoes and add the sugar. Simmer for about 5 minutes. Season with salt and pepper to taste and stir in the basil.

3. Add the pasta to the sauté pan with the sauce. Heat over medium heat for 1–2 minutes. If the sauce seems dry or is too thick, add some of the reserved cooking liquid. Serve with the mozzarella scattered on the top.

Emerald Pasta

This green-flecked pasta dish with a hint of lemon is easy elegance on a plate.

Prep & cook time (25 min)   Serves 4–6

- 1 **pound (450 g) tagliatelle or fettuccini**
- 2 **tablespoons olive oil, plus extra for tossing with the pasta**
- 1 **shallot, thinly sliced**
- 1 **cup (130 g) cubed zucchini**
- 1 **cup (115 g) frozen peas, thawed**

Salt and ground black pepper

- ¾ **cup (175 g) crumbled goat cheese**

Zest of 1 lemon

> *Swap It!*
> For a springtime treat, I like to toss in a handful of chopped-up asparagus stems in place of the zucchini.

1. Bring a pot of salted water to a boil. Add the pasta and boil for 8 minutes, until al dente, or cook according to the package directions. Reserve ½ cup (120 ml) of the cooking liquid and set aside. Drain the pasta and toss with just enough extra olive oil to keep it from sticking.

2. Return the pot to the stove and set over medium-high heat. Add the oil and heat for 30 seconds. Add the shallot and sauté for 2–3 minutes, stirring often. Add the zucchini and sauté for 2 minutes. Add the peas and a pinch of salt and sauté for 1–2 minutes, or until the peas and zucchini are heated through.

3. Add the pasta to the sauté pan with half of the reserved cooking liquid. Toss, coating the noodles with the sauce, and cook for 1–2 minutes. If too thick, add some of the remaining cooking liquid. Season with salt and pepper to taste and turn off the heat. Stir in the goat cheese and lemon zest and serve immediately.

Carbonara á la Kitty

Eggs, bacon, pasta—what could be better? The yolks in this version result in an extra creamy sauce. Mangia, mangia!

Prep & cook time 25 min | Serves 4–6

- **1   pound (450 g) linguini or spaghetti**
- **2   tablespoons olive oil, plus extra for tossing with the pasta**
- **4   large eggs, plus 2 yolks**
- **1   cup (115 g) grated Parmesan cheese, plus extra to garnish**
- **¹⁄₂ teaspoon red pepper flakes**
- **4   ounces (115 g) smoked bacon, cubed**
- **2   cloves garlic, smashed and peeled**
- **Salt and ground black pepper**

❶ Bring a pot of salted water to a boil. Add the pasta and boil for 8 minutes, until al dente, or cook according to the package directions. Reserve ½ cup (120 ml) of the cooking liquid and set aside. Drain the pasta and toss with just enough of the olive oil to keep it from sticking.

❷ Meanwhile, whisk together the eggs and cheese.

❸ Set the pot back on the stove over medium-high heat. Swirl in the olive oil along with the red pepper flakes, bacon, and garlic. Sauté for 5 minutes, until the bacon is slightly crispy. Discard the garlic.

❹ Add the pasta to the pot and cook, tossing to combine, for 1–2 minutes. Reduce the heat to low and pour in the eggs. Cook, stirring constantly (so they don't scramble), for 30–60 seconds, then turn off the heat. If the sauce is too thick, add some of the reserved cooking liquid.

❺ Season with salt and a good amount of black pepper to taste. Serve with grated Parmesan scattered on top.

One pan? Thank you, ma'am!

No-Fuss Meaty Rigatoni

Not all meat sauces are equal. Some take hours on the burner and others don't. Here's a recipe that has the right idea.

Prep & cook time | Serves 4–6

I   **pound (450 g) rigatoni**
I   **tablespoon olive oil, plus extra for tossing with the pasta**
I   **teaspoon fennel seeds**
2   **tablespoons tomato paste**
I   **pound (450 g) hot Italian sausage, removed from its casing (sliced open with a sharp knife) and crumbled**
I   **cup (240 ml) white wine**
Salt and ground black pepper
¾   **cup (175 ml) heavy cream**
3   **tablespoons mustard**
Chopped fresh parsley or basil to garnish (optional)

1. Bring a pot of salted water to a boil. Add the pasta and boil for 8 minutes, until al dente, or cook according to the package directions. Reserve ¹/₂ cup (120 ml) of the cooking liquid and set aside. Drain the pasta and toss with just enough extra olive oil to keep it from sticking.

2. Meanwhile, in a heavy sauté pan, heat the olive oil, fennel seeds, and tomato paste over medium-high heat. Add the sausage meat and cook for 5 minutes, until no longer pink, breaking up the meat with a spatula or spoon.

3. Stir in the wine and season with salt and pepper to taste. Simmer for 3–4 minutes, until the wine is reduced by half. Add the cream and mustard and simmer for 2 minutes.

4. Add the pasta to the sauté pan. Cook, stirring constantly, for 1–2 minutes. If too thick, add the reserved liquid. Scatter with chopped herbs, if you like, and serve.

MAIN DISHES

Cheater's Chili

A fuss-free, vegetarian meal that's good for a crowd. You'll need to stir occasionally, but otherwise let the simmering pot do the work while you kick back and relax.

Prep & cook time (1½ hr) | Serves 8–10

I	**large onion, quartered**
I	**carrot, cut into thirds**
6	**cloves garlic, smashed and peeled**
I	**jalapeño pepper, stem removed**
2	**tablespoons olive oil**
3	**tablespoons chili powder**
I	**teaspoon ground cumin**
⅛	**teaspoon cayenne pepper**
I	**28-ounce (800-g) can crushed tomatoes**
½	**teaspoon salt**
4	**cups (1 L) vegetable broth or water**
I	**15-ounce (425-g) can each kidney beans, cannellini beans, and pinto beans, drained and rinsed**

Salt and ground black pepper

1️⃣ Place the onion, carrot, garlic, and jalapeño pepper in a food processor. Pulse until coarsely chopped.

2️⃣ Heat the olive oil in a stockpot over medium heat and add the chopped vegetables. Sauté for about 10 minutes, until softened. Add the chili powder, cumin, and cayenne pepper and sauté for another minute.

3️⃣ Stir in the tomatoes, salt, broth, and beans. Bring to a boil. Reduce the heat and gently simmer for 1 hour, or until the chili has reached the desired consistency. Stir occasionally, checking that the beans don't stick to the bottom of the pot. Season with salt and pepper to taste.

Simply Stewed

Chorizo, chickpeas, spinach, and tomatoes make for a hearty meal—and will keep your diners coming back for more.

Prep & cook time Serves 4–6

1	8-ounce (225-g) link Spanish chorizo, sliced
2	tablespoons olive oil, plus extra for drizzling
2	onions, sliced
2	cloves garlic, smashed and peeled
	Salt and ground black pepper
1	tablespoon tomato paste
2	cups (475 ml) chicken or vegetable broth
½	cup (120 ml) water
2	14-ounce (400-g) cans chickpeas, drained and rinsed
10	ounces (275 g) fresh spinach
2	cups (300 g) cherry tomatoes, halved
	Crusty bread or rice to serve (optional)

1 Place a medium pot over medium heat. Add the chorizo and cook, stirring occasionally, for 2–3 minutes, until browned. Transfer the chorizo to a plate. Drain off all but ½ tablespoon of the fat and return the pan to the heat.

2 Add the oil, then add the onions and garlic, and season with salt and pepper. Sauté for about 7 minutes, until the onion softens. Stir in the tomato paste and cook, stirring, for 1–2 minutes, or until slightly darkened and fragrant.

3 Stir in the broth and water and bring to a boil. Reduce the heat and simmer for 2–3 minutes. Stir in the chickpeas, spinach, and chorizo and simmer for 5 minutes. Add the tomatoes and simmer for another 2 minutes. Season with salt and pepper. Top with a good drizzle of olive oil and serve with crusty bread or rice, if desired.

MAIN DISHES

Burger Bonanza

I can't decide which is my favorite, so here's a turkey, beef, and pork patty that you can slap on a toasted bun. Serve with all the fixings—lettuce, tomatoes, pickles, melted cheese, or … whatever. There's something for everyone.

Prep & cook time 15 min | Serves 4

1   **pound (450 g) ground beef**
¼   **teaspoon salt**
¼   **teaspoon ground black pepper**
2   **tablespoons olive oil**
4   **hamburger buns, split and toasted**
Choice of lettuce, sliced tomatoes, sliced onions, sliced pickles, cheese, ketchup, and other condiments to serve (optional)

1️⃣ Mix the beef, salt, and pepper together in a large mixing bowl. Divide the meat mixture into 4 equal portions. Using your hands, form four ¾-inch (2-cm) thick patties. Make a light thumbprint in the center of each—this will help to prevent it from arching while cooking. Sprinkle both sides with extra salt and pepper.

2️⃣ Heat a heavy, nonstick skillet over medium-high heat for about 1 minute. Once the pan is hot, swirl in the oil.

3️⃣ Lay the burgers in the pan 1-inch (2.5-cm) apart. Cook for about 5 minutes, until the bottom is seared and golden. Flip over with a spatula and cook for another 4 minutes, until seared and medium done.

HOT ENOUGH?

For a good burger, it must be seared in a hot skillet. To check if the skillet is hot enough before adding the burgers, I hold my hand about 1½ inches (4 cm) above the pan. If I can feel a strong heat, I know the pan is hot enough.

One pan? Thank you, ma'am!

TOTALLY TURKEY

Mix together 1½ pounds (675 g) of ground turkey (preferrably dark meat), ¼ teaspoon each of ground cumin and ground coriander, ¾ teaspoon of paprika, 2 tablespoons of mayonnaise, 1 teaspoon of fresh lemon juice, 1 clove of chopped garlic, ¼ teaspoon each of salt and ground black pepper, and 2 tablespoons of olive oil in a large mixing bowl. Shape into patties as described in Step 1 of the main recipe (see page 82).

Cook as described in Steps 2 and 3, but increase the cooking time to 6 minutes on the first side, until the bottom half is seared and golden. Then flip over the burgers and cook for 5 minutes, until seared and golden.

PERFECTLY PORKY

Mix together 1 pound (450 g) of ground pork, 2 tablespoons of chopped fresh parsley (or 2 teaspoons dried parsley), 1 tablespoon of Dijon mustard, 1 large egg, ¼ teaspoon each of salt and ground black pepper, and 2 tablespoons of olive oil in a large mixing bowl. Shape into patties as described in Step 1 of the main recipe (see page 82).

Cook as in Steps 2 and 3, but increase the cooking time to 6 minutes on the first side, or until the bottom half is seared and golden. Then flip over the burgers and cook for 5 minutes, or until seared and cooked through.

Life's too short to chop onions

Forget-Me-Not Chicken

Chicken gets bathed in a sweetly spiced sauce. Serve it with rice or potatoes and you've got true comfort food.

Prep & cook time Serves 4

2   **tablespoons butter**
2   **tablespoons olive oil**
1   **onion, thinly sliced**
4   **chicken breasts**
Salt and ground black pepper
1   **cinnamon stick**
¼   **teaspoon ground ginger**
1   **bay leaf**
1   **tablespoon honey**
1   **cup (175 g) dried apricots**
2   **cups (475 ml) chicken stock**
1   **cup (240 ml) white wine**
½   **cup (50 g) walnut halves**

1 Set a large sauté pan over a medium-high heat. Swirl in 1 tablespoon each of the butter and olive oil. When heated, stir in the onion. Reduce the heat to medium and cook for 8–10 minutes, until soft. Transfer the onion to a plate.

2 Add the remaining butter and olive oil to the pan. Season the chicken with salt and pepper. Put the chicken into the pan, skin side down, and sear for 3 minutes, then turn over and sear the other side for another 3 minutes.

3 Return the onion to the pan. Add the cinnamon, ginger, bay leaf, honey, apricots, chicken stock, and wine. Bring to a boil. Reduce the heat and gently simmer, covered, for 10 minutes. Stir in the walnuts and cook, uncovered, for another 5 minutes, or until the chicken is cooked through.

One pan? Thank you, ma'am!

Just-a-Few-Minutes Steak

Dinner is only minutes away when skirt steak is on the menu.
Finish off this inexpensive meal with a delicious salsa verde.
Your cooking skills will have your guests green with envy.

Prep & cook time | Serves 4

1¼ pounds (565 g) skirt steak
Salt and ground black pepper
2   cups (100 g) cilantro leaves
2   cloves garlic, smashed and peeled
1   jalapeño pepper, seeded
2   scallions, roughly chopped
1   tablespoon coarse salt
Juice and zest of 1 lime
1   cup (240 ml) plus 2 tablespoons olive oil

① Season both sides of the steak with plenty of salt and
pepper. Set aside while assembling the sauce.

② For the sauce, put the cilantro, garlic, jalapeño, scallions,
salt, and lime zest and juice into a food processor. Pulse
until the mixture is evenly chopped and granular. Scrape
the mixture into a serving bowl and stir in 1 cup (240 ml)
of the olive oil. Season with salt and pepper to taste.

③ In large sauté pan, heat the remaining olive oil over
medium-high heat for 30 seconds. Add the steak and sear
each side for 2–4 minutes, depending on the thickness of
the steak. When medium rare, the steak will give slightly
when prodded. Transfer the steak to a cutting board and
let stand for at least 5 minutes.

④ Slice the steak against the grain, arrange on a serving
platter, and serve with the green sauce spooned over
the top or alongside.

Beef with Broccoli

My version of a classic Chinese takeout dish is easy to put together. What's more, it calls for flavorful flank steak and is ready before any delivery is even close to arriving.

Prep & cook time, plus marinating time 20 min | Serves 4–6

- **3 tablespoons soy sauce**
- **1 tablespoon rice wine vinegar**
- **1 tablespoon oyster sauce**
- **3 cloves garlic, smashed, peeled, and chopped**
- **1 teaspoon red pepper flakes**
- **1 teaspoon sugar**
- **¼ teaspoon ground black pepper**
- **1¼ pounds (500 g) flank steak, cut across the grain into ½-inch (1-cm) strips**
- **1 tablespoon cornstarch**
- **1 tablespoon plus 1 teaspoon canola oil**
- **½ cup (120 ml) water**
- **2 cups (140 g) broccoli florets**
- **Salt**
- **Boiled or steamed white or brown rice to serve**

1 In a bowl, whisk together the soy sauce, vinegar, oyster sauce, garlic, red pepper flakes, sugar, and black pepper. Add the meat, toss to coat, and set aside for 15 minutes. Transfer the meat to a plate. Whisk the cornstarch into the marinade until smooth and set aside.

2 Heat 1 tablespoon of the canola oil in a large sauté pan set over high heat. Once the oil is hot, put the meat in the pan in a single layer (you may have to brown the meat in two batches) and brown on all sides, 2–3 minutes per side. Transfer the meat to a clean plate and set aside.

One pan? Thank you, ma'am!

3 Add the water to the pan and stir up any sediment sticking to the bottom with a wooden spoon. Add the broccoli and cook for 3–4 minutes, or until tender. Add the reserved marinade and stir briskly while bringing to a boil, for about 1 minute.

4 Return the meat to the pan and toss to coat. Sauté for 1–2 minutes, until heated through. Season with salt and black pepper to taste. Serve with boiled or steamed white or brown rice.

> *Swap It!*
>
> If you can't find oyster sauce, you can use hoisin sauce (look in the aisle in your grocery store that has Chinese ingredients) as a substitute.

VARIATION

CHICKEN AND SNAP PEA STIR-FRY

If you hate broccoli, here's another stir-fry: Whisk together 3 teaspoons each of cornstarch and rice wine vinegar with 1 teaspoon grated, fresh ginger. Add 1½ pounds (675 g) cubed, boneless chicken breast to the mixture; toss to coat.

In a separate bowl, whisk together 3 tablespoons of soy sauce, 2 tablespoons of oyster sauce, 1 teaspoon of sugar, and 3 tablespoons of water. Set aside.

In a sauté pan, heat 3 tablespoons of canola oil over high heat. Add ½ teaspoon of red pepper flakes and 1 smashed, peeled, and chopped garlic clove and cook for 1 minute, until golden. Add the chicken mixture and cook, stirring constantly, for 2 minutes, until the chicken whitens.

Add 8 ounces (225 g) of snap peas, stems removed, and cook for 2 minutes, until the peas are crisp-tender. Reduce the heat and add the soy sauce mixture. Cook, stirring, for 1 minute. Stir in ½ cup (55 g) cashew nuts and cook for 30 seconds. Serve with white rice.

MAIN DISHES

Luscious Lamb Stew

Don't let the long list of ingredients and cooking time scare you. Simply spend a few minutes assembling the dish, turn on the stove, and relax for a few hours.

Prep & cook time 3 hr | Serves 6

- 1 pound (450 g) stewing lamb, already cut into cubes
- 1½ tablespoons caraway seeds
- 1 tablespoon ground coriander
- 3 cloves garlic, smashed, peeled, and chopped
- ½ teaspoon cayenne pepper
- 3 tablespoons olive oil
- ½ tablespoon salt
- ¼ teaspoon ground black pepper
- 1 large onion, thinly sliced
- 1 bay leaf
- 2 tablespoons tomato paste
- 2 cups (475 ml) chicken stock
- ½ cup (120 ml) white wine
- ¼ cup (60 ml) lemon juice
- 1 cinnamon stick
- ¼ teaspoon allspice berries
- 1 14-ounce (400-g) can chickpeas, drained and rinsed
- 1 medium eggplant, cut into 1-inch (2.5-cm) cubes

1. Toss the lamb with the caraway seeds, coriander, garlic, cayenne pepper, 1 tablespoon of the olive oil, and the salt and black pepper.

2. Heat the remaining olive oil in a wide, heavy pot over a medium-high heat. Put the meat in the pot in a single layer. Brown the lamb on all sides. Stir in the onion, bay leaf, and tomato paste. Sauté for 7 minutes.

One pan? Thank you, ma'am!

③ Add the chicken stock, white wine, lemon juice, cinnamon stick, and allspice berries. Bring to a boil and reduce the heat to low. Cover the pot and simmer for 2½ hours.

④ Stir in the chickpeas and eggplant. Simmer for 15 minutes, until the eggplant is tender and chickpeas are well heated.

Destiny's Pork Chops

Pork and apples have got it going on. Put them together and get ready for some good eating.

Prep & cook time 25 min   Serves 4

2 tablespoons olive oil
4 pork chops, about ½-inch (1-cm) thick
1½ cups (350 ml) hard apple cider, apple juice, or cider
½ cup (120 ml) water
2 Granny Smith apples, cored and cut into ½-inch (1-cm) wedges
1 tablespoon light brown sugar
1 tablespoon butter
Salt and ground black pepper

① In a skillet, heat the olive oil over medium heat. Add the chops and cook for 4–5 minutes, until seared and golden. Turn over and cook for 4 minutes, until seared, golden, and cooked through. Transfer to a plate and keep warm.

② Add the cider and water to the skillet, stir up any sediment sticking to the bottom, and bring to a simmer. Stir in the apples and sugar. Simmer for 10 minutes, until the apples are tender. Stir in the butter and season with salt and pepper to taste. Spoon the sauce over the chops to serve.

MAIN DISHES

Herb-y Halibut

Fish and herbs combine to make a delicious dish that's as easy as pie. In fact, much easier than pie!

Prep & cook time 25 min | Serves 4

4   halibut fillets, about 5 ounces (150 g) each
Grated zest of I lemon
I   tablespoon fresh or I teaspoon dried herbes de Provence
I   tablespoon finely chopped fresh or I teaspoon dried parsley
¼   cup (60 ml) olive oil
Salt and ground black pepper
¼   cup (55 g) crème fraîche (see page 21) or sour cream
I   tablespoon lemon juice
I½ tablespoons snipped chives (optional)

1 Season the fish with the lemon zest, herbs, I tablespoon of the olive oil, salt, and black pepper. Cover and let stand for 15 minutes.

2 Heat a large sauté pan over a high heat for 2 minutes. Swirl 2 tablespoons of olive oil into the pan. When hot, after I minute, carefully put the fish in a single layer into the pan (cook in two batches, if necessary) and cook for 3–4 minutes, until seared and lightly browned. Turn over and reduce the heat to medium low. Cook for another 2–3 minutes, or until the fish flakes easily and the center is slightly translucent (it will continue to cook a little when removed from the pan). Drizzle with the remaining oil.

3 Meanwhile, make a sauce by mixing together the crème fraîche or sour cream with the lemon juice and season with salt and pepper to taste. Mix in the chives, if desired, and serve the sauce with the fish.

Scrumptious Shrimp

This dish is hard to mess up—just watch the shrimp so they don't overcook. Once they turn pink and curl up, stop cooking!

Prep & cook time | Serves 4–6

½   **red onion, thinly sliced**
2   **tablespoons red wine vinegar**
Salt and ground black pepper
5   **tablespoons olive oil**
2   **cloves garlic, sliced**
2   **1-inch (2.5 cm) strips of orange peel**
¼   **teaspoon paprika**
¼   **teaspoon cumin**
1   **pound (450 g) raw shrimp, preshelled and deveined**
1   **14-ounce (400-g) can chickpeas, drained and rinsed**
Cilantro leaves or flat-leaf parsley to garnish (optional)

1 Place the onions and vinegar in a medium bowl and season with salt and pepper. Toss to coat and set aside.

2 In a large sauté pan, heat 2 tablespoons of the olive oil over medium heat. Add the garlic, orange peel, paprika, and cumin and sauté for 1–2 minutes, until the garlic turns golden. Add the shrimp and chickpeas to the pan, and sauté, stirring constantly, for 2–3 minutes, until the shrimp and chickpeas are just cooked through.

3 Transfer the shrimp and chickpeas to the bowl with the onion and toss to combine. Add the remaining oil and toss again, and season with salt and pepper to taste. Garnish with the cilantro leaves or parsley, if desired.

SIDE DISHES

Snappy Peas

Vegetable nirvana: These sugar snap peas don't need to be shucked—save your fingers for more important things.

Prep & cook time 10 min | Serves 4

I   **tablespoon olive oil**
I   **pound (450 g) sugar snap peas, stems removed**
¼   **cup (12.5 g) chopped mint**
Grated zest of ½ lemon
I   **tablespoon lemon juice**
Salt and ground black pepper

1 Heat the olive oil in a sauté pan over medium-high heat for 1 minute. Add the sugar snap peas and sauté for 3–5 minutes, until crisp and tender. Turn off the heat.

2 Stir in the mint, lemon zest, and lemon juice. Season with salt and pepper to taste.

SNAPPY RICE
I use this recipe to transform ordinary white rice. Cut the peas in half before sautéing, and when done toss with cooked rice, adding more lemon zest, salt, or oil to taste.

One pan? Thank you, ma'am!

Jalapeño-Butter Corn

Corn is good, eaten from the cob or spooned from a bowl, but butter, jalapeño, and cilantro make it better still. If only everything were this easy.

Prep & cook time | Serves 4

4 **ears of corn, husks removed**
2 **jalapeño peppers, stem removed (to avoid a spicy butter, remove the seeds and membrane)**
¼ cup (15 g) cilantro leaves
3 **tablespoons unsalted butter, at room temperature**
½ teaspoon salt
Lime wedges to serve (optional)

1. Bring a large pot of water to a boil. Add the corn and cook for 4–5 minutes. Drain and set the corn aside.

2. In a food processor, pulse the jalapeño peppers and cilantro until finely chopped. Add the butter and salt and pulse until well blended.

3. Smear the corn with the butter, or transfer the butter to small dishes and serve alongside the corn. Serve with lime wedges, if desired, and extra salt.

> *Swap It!*
>
> For an easier version, swap the fresh ears of corn for 2½ cups (400 g) of thawed, frozen corn kernels. Sauté the corn with half of the butter mixture (this brings out the heat and flavor of the jalapeño-cilantro butter). Add more butter, salt, or lime juice to taste. Or for the best flavor, but more work, slice the kernels off the cob.

SIDE DISHES

Smashed Red Potatoes

So good. So rich. So satisfying. The only thing these potatoes are not is so-so.

 Prep & cook time **30 min** | Serves 4

6   **tablespoons unsalted butter**
1½ pounds (675 g) red new potatoes, quartered
5   **medium garlic cloves, smashed and peeled**
1   **cup (240 ml) water**
¼ cup (60 ml) heavy cream, plus extra if needed
Salt and ground black pepper

1. Melt the butter in a medium pot. Add the potatoes, garlic, and water. Bring to a simmer, cover, and cook gently for 20 minutes, or until the potatoes are velvety and fork tender.

2. In a microwave oven set on high, warm the cream for 30–40 seconds, or until steaming.

3. Remove the pan from the heat and mash the potatoes with a potato masher. Stir in the hot cream. Heat and add more cream if you want a thinner mash. Season with salt and pepper to taste.

Swap It!

For a smooth mash (but more work), use 1½ pounds (675 g) diced russet potatoes instead of the new potatoes. You can also add a pinch of nutmeg to the cream or 2 tablespoons of crème fraîche (see page 21) or sour cream.

Popeye Loves Olive Oil

The food of champions made simple. Eat up.

Prep & cook time | Serves 4

3 **tablespoons olive oil**
½ **bulb of garlic (cut the bulb through the middle)**
1 **pound (450 g) fresh spinach leaves, washed and drained, but with water still clinging to the leaves**
Salt and ground black pepper

1 In a sauté pan, heat 2 tablespoons of the olive oil over a medium heat. Put the garlic, cut side down, into the pan and cook for 1–2 minutes, or until lightly browned.

2 Remove the garlic and discard. Add the spinach, cover, and cook for 1 minute. Uncover and cook, stirring, for 2 minutes, until all the leaves are wilted. Turn off the heat and strain off any excess water. Season with salt and pepper to taste. Add the remaining oil, toss, and serve warm.

VARIATION

PASTA WITH SPINACH AND SAUSAGE

Another side dish moves to center stage. After sautéing the spinach in the pan in Step 2, set it aside and clean out the pan. Remove the meat in an Italian sausage from its casing (use a sharp knife to slice open the casing) and fry the meat until no longer pink. Toss the sausage and spinach with a cooked pasta of your choice, such as bow ties, penne, or shells, and top with grated Parmesan cheese.

~ FOUR ~

Dessert in a dash!

Baked fruit and tarts and cookies ... oh my! Although
making desserts from scratch may sound scary,
take it from me: It's easy—and the rewards are sweet.
(Even the mistakes are usually edible.) Better yet,
your kitchen will be filled with wonderful aromas that
will make you feel like a domestic diva. (Go ahead,
throw on an apron and complete the look).

Did you know that according to studies, the scent
most likely to turn a man on is pumpkin spice? It's true.
Really. So you also need to believe me when I tell you
that the desserts here are easy to prepare. Sure, they
look and taste impressive, but they really only take the
culinary skills of a fifth grader to pull off. Of course,
no one needs to know that, least of all the guy who just
followed his nose to your kitchen door.

DESSERTS

Berries with Honeyed Mascarpone

This dessert highlights one of mascarpone's appealing attributes: No whipping required! Just add a touch of sweetener—honey works very well—and serve.

Prep & cook time Serves 4–6

1½ pints (12 oz–1¼ lb/350–500 g) berries (raspberries, blackberries, and/or blueberries)
2 tablespoons sugar
Juice of ½ lemon
8 ounces (225 g) mascarpone
3 tablespoons honey
Almond or butter cookies to serve (optional)

1 In a medium bowl, toss together the berries with the sugar and lemon juice. Set aside for 5 minutes, or until the berries release some of their juices.

2 In a separate small bowl, mix the mascarpone with the honey.

3 Spoon the berries into a serving bowl or individual glasses. Top with a dollop of the honeyed mascarpone. If you like, serve with an almond or butter cookie.

Swap It!

In a peachy mood? Replace the berries with 4 pitted, sliced peaches, and toss with ½ cup (120 ml) of white wine instead of the lemon juice and enough sugar to taste.

Baked Figs with Mascarpone

All you do is spread out the fruit and top with cheese. Much better than store-bought fig bars.

Prep & cook time | Serves 6

12	**fresh figs**
2	**tablespoons sugar**
2	**tablespoons honey**
8	**ounces (225 g) mascarpone**
I	**tablespoon rum**

Raspberry sorbet to serve (optional)

1. Preheat the oven to 375°F (190°C). Remove the stems from the figs and halve them lengthwise. Place them, cut side up, so they fit snugly in a medium baking dish.

2. In a separate small bowl, whisk together I tablespoon of the sugar, the honey, mascarpone, and rum. Spread the mascarpone mixture evenly over the figs, and then sprinkle the remaining sugar over the top.

3. Bake in the preheated oven for 15 minutes, or until browned in spots. Remove from the oven and let cool slightly. To serve, place the warm figs in small bowls and add a small scoop of sorbet alongside, if you like.

Apricots Meet Vanilla

Apricots and vanilla make a great combo, and using fresh vanilla is easier than you think. Make this recipe ahead of time, so you can still have a nice dessert on a crazy, busy day.

Prep & cook time, plus chilling Serves 6

- ¾ **cup sugar**
- ½ **vanilla bean**
- 1 **cup (240 ml) Sauternes, or another white dessert wine**
- 2 **cups (475 ml) water**
- 1 **pound (450 g) apricots (about 8–10), washed, halved, and pits removed**

1. Put the sugar in a small bowl. With a sharp knife, halve the ½ vanilla bean lengthwise. Splay open the bean and hold down the sides with your fingertips. Run the knife tip inside the bean, carefully scraping up the tiny seeds as you go. Scrape all the seeds into the bowl of sugar and combine together. (Do not discard the bean.)

2. Transfer the vanilla-sugar mixture and the vanilla bean to a saucepan. Add the Sauternes and water. Turn the heat to medium high and bring to a boil. Add the apricots and reduce the heat to medium low. Simmer for 3–5 minutes, or until the apricots are easily pierced with the tip of a knife.

3. Remove the apricots from the heat and let cool in the cooking liquid. Chill in the refrigerator for 2 hours, but preferably overnight. They will keep for up to 5 days.

Swap It!

If fresh apricots are out of season, there's no need to lose hope. Use 8 ounces (225 g) dried apricots instead and cook as directed above for 30 minutes, or until the dried fruit is soft and full.

Dessert in a dash!

Peachy Granola Crumble

Warm fruit with a buttery, oat topping is delicious, and after a few minutes of assembling, you can catch up on your favorite soap or sitcom as it bakes.

Prep & cook time | Serves 6

3   ripe peaches, pitted and quartered
½   pint (6 ounces/170 g) blackberries
Juice of ½ lemon
½   cup (100 g) sugar
6   tablespoons butter, at room temperature
1½ cups (175 g) granola, with almonds or pecans
2   tablespoons flour
Vanilla ice cream (to serve)

1. Preheat the oven to 375°F (190°C). In a mixing bowl, gently toss together the peaches and blackberries with the lemon juice and half of the sugar. Put the mixture into a medium ovenproof dish.

2. For the topping, put the butter, granola, remaining sugar, and flour in a mixing bowl or food processor. Rub the mixture together with your fingers, or pulse, until crumbly. Sprinkle the mixture evenly over the fruit.

3. Bake in the preheated oven for 30 minutes, or until the fruit is bubbling and the top is golden and has browned in spots. Serve with a scoop of vanilla ice cream.

Life's too short to chop onions

DESSERTS

Pass-It-On Apricot Tart

This no-roll, foolproof pie dough lives up to the expression "easy as pie." The recipe reached me after being passed on from a friend to a friend to a friend …

Prep & cook time 55 min | Serves 6

|---|---|
8	tablespoons (1 stick/115 g) unsalted butter, melted
¼	cup (50 g) sugar, plus extra for sprinkling
¼	teaspoon salt
¾	cup (100 g) flour
¼	cup (30 g) ground almonds or oats
1	cup (275 g) apricot jam

1 Preheat the oven to 350°F (180°C). In a medium bowl, mix together the butter, sugar, salt, flour, and ground almonds or oats. Let the dough stand for 1–2 minutes.

2 Transfer the dough to a 9-inch (23-cm) tart pan with a removable bottom. Press the dough evenly across the bottom and up the sides, pressing well into the corners. Bake for 20 minutes, or until golden brown. Check halfway through baking. If the dough is puffing up, gently prick the bottom where it's puffy with a fork. Once golden brown, remove the tart crust from the oven and let stand on a wire rack for 10 minutes, until cool.

3 Increase the oven heat to 425°F (220°C). Evenly spread the jam across the crust. Sprinkle a little sugar over the top and return to the oven. Bake for 10 minutes, or until slightly caramelized and browned on the edges.

Swap It!
Apricot jam not your fave? Any jam will do, such as raspberry. Or brush the baked pie crust with melted chocolate and arrange fresh fruit over the top. Try to top that!

Chocolate Chip Cookies

Even if you hate to bake, perhaps knowing that in only about 15 minutes you'll have world-class cookies ready to bake might change your mind. Now it's your turn to wear a milk mustache!

Prep & cook time | Yields 24

- ⅓ **cup (65 g) granulated sugar**
- ⅓ **cup (75 g) firmly packed light brown sugar**
- 10 **tablespoons (1¼ sticks/150 g) unsalted butter, cut into ½-inch (1-cm) pieces**
- 1 **large egg**
- 1 **teaspoon vanilla extract**
- 1¼ **cups (160 g) all-purpose flour**
- ¼ **teaspoon baking soda**
- ½ **teaspoon salt**
- 1½ **cups (225 g) semisweet chocolate chips**
- ¾ **cup (90 g) chopped pecans or walnuts**

1 Preheat the oven to 325°F (160°C). Move the oven rack to the top third of the oven. Line two cookie sheets with parchment paper.

2 In a mixing bowl, beat together the granulated sugar, brown sugar, and butter until smooth, using an electric mixer. Mix in the egg and vanilla extract.

3 In a separate bowl, sift together the flour, baking soda, and salt. Stir the flour mixture into the batter until just combined. Stir in the chocolate chips and nuts.

4 Scoop the cookie dough into 2-tablespoon balls and arrange them 4 inches (10 cm) apart on the cookie sheets. Bake for 18 minutes, or until golden brown and slightly soft in the center. Remove from the oven and let cool on a wire rack.

DESSERTS

Ebony and Ivory Cookies

Rich and comforting—all a cookie (and your dream guy) could be. Better yet, you can make the dough ahead of time, store in the refrigerator until needed, then bake and serve warm!

Prep & cook time, plus chilling Yields 24

- **12 tablespoons (1½ sticks/175 g) unsalted butter**
- **½ cup (100 g) granulated sugar**
- **¼ teaspoon salt**
- **½ teaspoon vanilla extract**
- **1 cup (125 g) all-purpose flour**
- **½ cup (50 g) unsweetened cocoa**
- **1 teaspoon baking soda**
- **1½ cups (225 g) white chocolate chips**

> *Swap It!*
> Use dark chocolate chips instead of white if you have less of a sweet tooth and want a real chocoholic experience.

1. In a mixing bowl, cream the butter until smooth, using an electric mixer set on medium speed. Add the sugar, salt, and vanilla extract and beat until smooth.

2. In a separate bowl, mix together the flour, cocoa, and baking soda. Stir the flour mixture into the butter mixture until just combined. Stir in the chocolate chips.

3. Divide the dough in half, shape the halves into 1½-inch (4-cm)-thick logs, and wrap in plastic wrap. Refrigerate the dough for at least 1 hour, or until firm.

4. Preheat the oven to 325°F (160°C). Line 2 cookie sheets with parchment paper. Unwrap the dough and slice the logs into ½-inch (1-cm) rounds. Space them 1 inch (2.5 cm) apart on the cookie sheets. Bake in the middle of the oven for 7 minutes, or until the edges are set but the center is still soft. Let cool on the sheets for 5 minutes and serve warm, or transfer to wire racks to cool completely.

Peanut Butter and Choc

To make something amazing even better, a piece of chocolate is put smack dab in the center of a peanut butter cookie.

Prep & cook time | Yields 24

6 tablespoons unsalted butter
¼ cup (50 g) granulated sugar
½ cup (100 g) packed, light brown sugar
½ teaspoon vanilla extract
1 cup (260 g) creamy peanut butter
1 large egg
1 ¼ cup (160 g) all-purpose flour
½ teaspoon baking powder
½ teaspoon salt
24 flattened, tear-shape chocolates or
solid, bite-size chocolate pieces

❶ Preheat the oven to 350°F (180°C). Line 2 cookie sheets with parchment paper. In a mixing bowl, beat together the butter, sugars, vanilla extract, and peanut butter for 2 minutes, or until combined, using an electric mixer set on low speed. Beat in the egg until just combined.

❷ In a separate bowl, sift together the flour, baking powder, and salt. Add the dry ingredients to the peanut butter mixture and beat until just combined.

❸ Roll the dough into 1-inch (2.5-cm) balls and space them 3 inches (7.5 cm) apart on the baking sheets, pressing down on each ball just enough to secure it on the sheet; do not completely flatten. Bake for 8–10 minutes, until the cookies are crispy on the edges and soft in the center. Transfer to a rack. While still warm, press 1 chocolate piece into the center of each cookie, then let cool.

~ FIVE ~

Easy entertaining

OK, sometimes it's not enough just to cook for yourself.
You'll have to feed other people, too. When performance
anxiety strikes, just reach for this chapter. Sure, you
could try other time-tested anxiety reducers. Public
speakers often try to calm down by imagining their
audiences naked. But let's be realistic: Thinking about
your dinner guests naked won't make you a better cook.
In fact, it might cause serious appetite loss, resulting
in an inability to cook anything at all.

Instead, follow these foolproof steps to easy entertaining.
You'll feel like a successful television-network chef as
you serve up amazing dishes to rounds of applause. (You
can keep that part of the fantasy alive, anyway!)

Camembert in a Box

Forget about brie, fumbling with pastry dough, or any of that nonsense. This is the real deal. Just one caution: Buy the Camembert in a box that is stapled, not glued.

Prep & cook time Serves 4–6

I	**8-or 9-ounce (225–250-g) round of Camembert cheese in a wooden box**
½	**bulb of garlic (cut it through the middle)**
I–2	**tablespoons white wine**
I	**baguette or loaf of crusty country bread, sliced and toasted, to serve**

1 Preheat the oven to 400°F (200°C) and line a baking sheet with parchment paper. Remove the Camembert from its box and discard the wrapping. Rub the rind with the cut side of the garlic head.

2 Put the cheese back into the bottom half of the box and place on the lined baking sheet. With the tip of a knife, poke 10 small holes through the top rind. Sprinkle the cheese with 1–2 tablespoons of the wine. Place the top of the box back over the cheese and bake for 15 minutes, or until soft, warm, and bubbling.

3 To serve, remove the top of the box and place the cheese on a serving plate. Serve with the toasted bread.

VARIATION

SWEET BOX

Omit the garlic and wine. Drizzle with 1 tablespoon of honey, scatter 1 teaspoon thyme leaves over the top, and bake as directed.

Cucumber-Avocado Soup

A spa-style soup you can make ahead of time and have ready in minutes. Who says you don't have time for a facial when you're throwing a dinner party?

Prep & cook time, plus chilling 15 min | Serves 4

2 garlic cloves, smashed and peeled
I large cucumber, peeled, halved, and seeds removed with the tip of a spoon
I large ripe avocado, halved, pitted, and peeled
I cup (240 ml) buttermilk
2 tablespoons fresh dill (or basil)
Juice of I–2 limes
Salt and ground black pepper

1 Add the garlic, cucumber, and avocado to a food processor. Puree until smooth, pausing to scrape down the sides as necessary.

2 Add the buttermilk, dill, juice of I lime, and a pinch of salt and pepper. Blend until smooth.

3 Taste and adjust the seasoning, adding more salt, pepper, and lime juice, if needed. If the soup seems too thick, add a little water to thin it to the desired consistency. Cover and refrigerate for at least I hour, until well chilled. Serve cold.

SPRUCE IT UP

Garnish the soup with 2 or 3 cooked shrimp tossed with a drizzle of olive oil, some chopped dill, and salt and pepper. Or halve a handful of cherry tomatoes and toss them with a little chopped basil, half a cubed avocado, a drizzle of oil, and some salt and pepper. Violà—you have a foodie-friendly soup.

No-Cook Crab Salad

A crabby salad that makes the cook anything but …

Prep & cook time | Serves 4–6

I	**pound (450 g) fresh, picked crabmeat**
2	**scallions, white and light green parts only, thinly sliced**
¼	**cup (12 g) roughly chopped, fresh cilantro leaves**

Juice and grated zest of 1–2 limes

5	**tablespoons olive oil**

Salt and ground black pepper

3–4 Belgian endives, stems removed and leaves separated

1 In a bowl, lightly toss the crabmeat with all of the ingredients except for the endive. Taste for seasoning and adjust with salt, pepper, oil, zest or juice, if desired.

2 Serve with the endive leaves alongside for scooping up the crab salad.

Swap It!

For a creamier salad, substitute either mayonnaise or sour cream for the oil. Use just enough to bind together the crabmeat—you'll find that 4–6 tablespoons will be enough.

Sensational Roasted Shrimp

Salt roasting may be popular among gourmets, but its simplicity will have you hooked. Despite the salt, these won't taste salty (see below).

Prep & cook time 15 min | Serves 4–6

2–2½	**pounds (900 g–1.2 kg) kosher salt**
16	**shrimp (about 1 pound/450 g), raw and unpeeled**
4	**tablespoons butter, melted, to serve (optional)**
2	**lemons, cut into wedges, to serve (optional)**

1. Preheat the oven to 450°F (230°C).

2. On a baking sheet that comfortably fits the shrimp in a single layer, spread out the salt, covering the bottom in a thick layer. Arrange the shrimp over the salt and gently press them into it.

3. Bake for 6–7 minutes, until the shrimp is just opaque in the center and the shells are pink. Serve the shrimp on a platter with the melted butter and lemon wedges, if using, alongside.

What's That?

Salt roasting is a great technique in which you bury food in a mound of salt before roasting in the oven. The salt seals the food, intensifies the heat, and extracts moisture, but it doesn't leave your dish tasting salty. In fact, the technique brings out the flavors of most ingredients.

Chicken Legs with Cream and Leeks

*Luxurious, cheap, and made in one dish. Sounds great? It is.
If only other things in life were this simple.*

Prep & cook time 1¾ hr | Serves 4

4   **large chicken leg-thigh parts**

**Grated zest of 2 lemons, plus 1–2 tablespoons
    lemon juice (optional)**

Salt and ground black pepper

2   **tablespoons olive oil**

1   **tablespoon butter**

4   **medium leeks, white and light green parts only, cut into
    rounds, and soaked, rinsed, and drained in a colander**

3   **tablespoons chopped fresh or 1 tablespoon dried thyme**

2   **cups (475 ml) white wine**

¼   **cup (60 ml) crème fraîche (see page 21) or sour cream**

❶ Let the chicken come to room temperature and season
with the lemon zest, salt, and pepper.

❷ Set a Dutch oven or deep, heavy pot over medium-
high heat and swirl in the olive oil and butter. Once the
butter melts, lay the chicken, skin side down, into the pot.
Cook, undisturbed, for 3–4 minutes, or until the skin is a
deep brown. (If the pot isn't big enough, you may have to
do this in two batches.) Turn over the chicken and cook
for another 3–4 minutes, or until golden brown. Transfer
the legs to a large plate and pour off the fat.

❸ Add the leeks to the pot and sauté for 1–2 minutes,
stirring and scraping up any browned sediment stuck
to the bottom. Stir in the thyme and sauté for another
1 minute. Add the wine and boil for 5 minutes, or until

the alcohol has burned off (taste or sniff to tell if the bitter alcohol taste is gone).

④ Return the chicken legs to the pot, arranging them skin side up over the leeks (if you cannot fit them in one layer, overlap them slightly). Reduce the heat to medium low. Cover and gently simmer for about 1 hour, or until the chicken is cooked through and tender.

⑤ Transfer the chicken to a serving platter. Stir the crème fraîche or sour cream into the pot with the leeks and cook for 5 minutes, or until the sauce thickens slightly. Season with salt and pepper and a squirt of lemon juice, if desired. Spoon the sauce over and around the chicken.

VARIATIONS

SPRINGTIME CHICKEN WITH ASPARAGUS

Cut off the fibrous stem ends from a 1-pound (450-g) bunch of asparagus. Slice the asparagus, on the diagonal, into 3-inch (7.5-cm) lengths. In step 5, after removing the chicken, add the asparagus to the leeks and cook for 2 minutes. Then add the cream, as directed, and cook for 5 minutes or until the asparagus is crisp-tender.

WINTERTIME CHICKEN WITH BACON

For a more substantial winter version, add 4 ounces (115 g) of bacon, cut into bite-size pieces. Before adding the leeks in step 3, add the bacon and brown on all sides, about 2 minutes for each side. Pour off the fat, add the leeks, and proceed as directed.

Figs Gone A-Fowl

This recipe is as straightforward as it gets. You could say that it was catered, and no one would "fig-"ure it out.

Prep & cook time 1¼ hr | Serves 4

1	tablespoon juniper berries
½	tablespoon fresh thyme leaves, plus 20 sprigs
4	Muscovy duck breasts

Salt and ground black pepper
3–4 bay leaves

16	ripe figs, stems removed and halved lengthwise
1	tablespoon olive oil
1	cup (240 ml) port
½	cup (120 ml) balsamic vinegar

1. Preheat the oven to 400°F (200°C). Using a grinder, finely grind the juniper berries and thyme leaves. With a sharp knife, make shallow slashes into the fat on the breasts, but not the meat. Season with salt and pepper, then rub with the juniper mixture. Cover; let it reach room temperature.

2. Scatter half the thyme sprigs and bay leaves in a baking dish. Add the figs, skin side up, and drizzle with oil. Add the remaining thyme and bay leaves. Bake for 20 minutes.

3. Place the breasts, skin side down, in a roasting pan and bake for 15 minutes. Remove from the oven and pour off the fat. Turn over the breasts and bake for 15–20 minutes, or until a meat thermometer reaches 135°F (57°C), for medium rare. Let the breasts rest for 10 minutes.

4. In a saucepan, bring the port and vinegar to a boil. Reduce the heat to medium low and cook for 5 minutes, or until reduced by a half. Thinly slice the duck crosswise and serve with the figs and sauce.

Bistro Steak with Blue Cheese

When ingredients suit each other like red meat and blue cheese do, just sit back and enjoy the compliments.

Prep & cook time 30 min | Serves 4

4 ounces (115 g) blue cheese, crumbled
7 tablespoons butter, softened
Salt
2 tablespoons cracked peppercorns, plus extra for seasoning
1 tablespoon chopped fresh or 1 teaspoon dried rosemary
2 tablespoons olive oil
4 steaks, 10 ounces (275 g) each and 1½ inches (4 cm) thick, such as New York strip, rib eye, or tri-tip

1 In a bowl, mix the blue cheese with 5 tablespoons of butter to make a smooth paste. Season with salt and peppercorns. Shape the flavored butter into a 4-inch (10-cm) log on wax paper and wrap it. Refrigerate for 30 minutes, or until firm.

2 In a small grinder, coarsely grind together the rosemary and peppercorns. Pat the steaks dry with paper towels, season both sides with salt, then rub the peppercorn mixture evenly over the steak. Set the steaks aside, covered, until they reach room temperature.

3 Place a large, heavy skillet over high heat. Swirl in the remaining butter and the oil. Once hot, lay the steaks into the skillet and sear for 4 minutes, until browned, occasionally spooning the butter mixture on top. Turn the steaks over and cook for 3–4 minutes for medium rare. Transfer to a cutting board and let rest for 10 minutes.

4 Scrape up any sediment on the bottom of the pan and stir the juices. Transfer the steaks to serving plates, pour the juices over, and top with a pat of blue-cheese butter.

My Mom's Lamb Roast

My mother is allergic to the kitchen. Here is her standby wine-and-dine dish.

Prep & cook time 1½ hr | Serves 4–6

1   **3-pound (1.3-kg) lamb shoulder, tied into a roast**
Salt and ground black pepper
3   **cloves garlic, peeled and sliced**
10 **sprigs fresh rosemary, plus 1 tablespoon, chopped**
10 **sprigs fresh thyme, plus 1 tablespoon, chopped**
Grated zest of 1 large lemon
½   **cup (120 ml) olive oil**
1   **cup (240 ml) white wine**

1 Preheat the oven to 375°F (190°C). Season the lamb all over with salt and pepper. Insert the garlic slices into the open flaps on the underside of the lamb. Scatter the sprigs of rosemary and thyme in a deep roasting pan and place the lamb on top.

2 Mix together the chopped herbs, lemon zest, and olive oil. Rub the mixture over the lamb, then pour over the wine. Transfer to the oven and roast for 45–50 minutes, or until the lamb is medium rare on the inside and crusty on the outside. (A meat thermometer should register 135°F/57°C). Put the lamb on a plate and let rest, undisturbed, for at least 15 minutes.

3 Remove the herb sprigs and scrape up any sediment stuck to the bottom of the pan. Pour the pan sauce through a strainer. Slice the lamb, and serve it with the the pan sauce passed around separately.

Pork with Rosemary and Sage

Meet your secret weapon in the kitchen: the pork tenderloin.

Prep & cook time | Serves 4–6

1½ pounds (675 g) pork tenderloin
1½ teaspoons dried fennel seeds, crushed in a grinder
Salt and ground black pepper
2   tablespoons olive oil
½   cup (120 ml) white wine
4   medium cloves garlic, smashed and peeled
3   sprigs each rosemary and sage

1 Preheat the oven to 350°F (180°C); set the rack in the center. Pat the pork dry with paper towels. Rub the fennel all over the pork and season with salt and pepper.

2 In a heatproof sauté pan, heat the oil over medium-high heat. Add the pork, brown for 5 minutes on each side, and set aside. Add the wine to the pan, stir up any sediment, and cook for 1–2 minutes. Add the garlic and sauté until lightly browned. Turn off the heat.

3 Lay half the herb sprigs in the pan and put the pork on top. Press the remaining sprigs across the pork. Roast in the oven for 10 minutes, or until a thermometer reads 150°F (65.5°C). Let rest for 10 minutes, slice, and serve.

RELISH THE MOMENT

With a masher, crush 1 cup (100 g) seedless red grapes in a bowl. Stir in ½ cup (50 g) of chopped, toasted almonds, 2 tablespoons of chopped fresh parsley, and 6 tablespoons of olive oil. Season with salt, black pepper, and a little lemon juice. Set aside for 10 minutes, or make up to an hour ahead; serve with the pork.

Take-a-Break Pea Risotto

Stir? Risotto? No need! To prove the point, make this recipe.

Prep & cook time 35 min | Serves 4–6

¼   **cup (60 ml) extra virgin olive oil**
1   **shallot, peeled and pulsed finely in a food processor**
2   **cloves garlic, peeled and pulsed in a food processor**
2   **cups (400 g) Arborio rice**
1½   **cup (350 ml) white wine**
3½   **cups (850 ml) vegetable or chicken broth or water**
1   **cup (25 g) loosely packed fresh basil**
1   **cup (100 g) Parmesan cheese, plus extra to garnish**
3   **cups (400 g) frozen peas, thawed**
¼   **cup (35 g) pine nuts**
Grated zest of 1 lemon
Salt and ground black pepper

1. Preheat the oven to 375°F (190°C). In a heavy heatproof pot, heat half the olive oil over medium heat. Add the shallot and cook for 4 minutes, until translucent. Add the garlic and cook for 1 minute. Add the rice and stir for 3 minutes. Stir in the wine and cook for 3–4 minutes. Mix in the broth or water, cover, and bake for 25 minutes.

2. Put the basil, half the cheese, 1 cup (135 g) of the peas, the pine nuts, and lemon zest into a food processor. Pulse until it forms a coarse pesto. Transfer to a bowl and stir in the remaining oil. Season with salt and pepper; set aside.

3. Remove the risotto from the oven, stir in the remaining peas, re-cover, and bake for 5 minutes, or until the rice is just tender but still firm. Stir in the remaining cheese and the reserved pesto. Taste and adjust the seasoning. Serve drizzled with olive oil and with extra grated Parmesan.

Polenta (aka Grits)

Creamy cornmeal, plain or dressed up, warms the soul. It goes well with shrimp, chicken, pork, mushrooms—you name it—making it the perfect side for just about any dinner party.

Prep & cook time 15 min | Serves 6–8

- **2 cups (240 ml) chicken, fish, or vegetable broth**
- **2 cups (240 ml) water**
- **1 cup (115 g) instant cornmeal**
- **½ cup (110 g) mascarpone cheese**
- **½ cup grated Parmesan cheese**
- **2 tablespoons olive oil**
- **Salt and ground black pepper**

1. Bring the broth and water to a boil in a saucepan. Reduce the heat to medium low. Whisk the cornmeal into the simmering liquid in a slow, steady stream. Switch to a wooden spoon and continue stirring, making sure the cornmeal doesn't stick to the bottom of the pan, for another 8–10 minutes. (This takes a little effort but it's not difficult. Really.)

2. The cornmeal is ready when it's thick, creamy, and tastes fully cooked. Remove from the heat and stir in the mascarpone, Parmesan, and olive oil. Season with salt and pepper to taste before serving.

> **STRESS-FREE PLANNING**
> Make polenta a few hours ahead of time, when you're relaxed. Cover it with plastic wrap and set aside. When you're ready to reheat the polenta, loosen it with a little water, then stir it until smooth and heated through. Best point yet: Polenta retains heat for a long time, so you can give more attention to the main course.

Winning Wild Rice

A far cry from rice in a bag, my friends love it every time.
Best of all, wild rice is hard to mess up.

Prep & cook time **40 min** | Serves 4

4 cups (1 L) water
1 bay leaf
1 1-inch (2.5-cm) strip of lemon peel
1 cup (160 g) wild rice, rinsed and dried
¾ cup (180 g) hazelnuts or almonds
¼ cup (60 ml) olive oil, plus extra for drizzling
Salt and ground black pepper
1 tablespoon lemon juice
¼ cup (12 g) chopped parsley

❶ Preheat the oven to 350°F (180°C). Put the water, bay leaf, and lemon peel in a medium saucepan and bring to a boil. Reduce the heat to medium low and stir in the rice. Simmer, uncovered, for 35 minutes, or until the rice is just tender. Drain the rice in a colander and toss to dry. Discard the bay leaf and lemon peel.

❷ Meanwhile, spread out the hazelnuts or almonds, in a single layer, in a small baking dish. Drizzle the nuts with oil and sprinkle on a little salt. Bake for 10 minutes, or until golden, then coarsely pulse in a food processor.

❸ To make a dressing, mix together the olive oil, lemon juice, salt, and pepper. Toss the rice with the nuts and parsley. Pour the dressing over the rice and toss to combine. Adjust the seasoning to taste. Serve warm or at room temperature.

Salt-Roasted Potatoes

Dump salt onto a roasting tray and place the food on top. That's it. When food is this simple, you have time for other things, such as sauces (nothing too involved, of course).

Prep & cook time Serves 4

3   pounds (1.3 kg) kosher salt
16 small potatoes, such as red bliss
Salt and ground black pepper
Juice of I lemon
½ cup (112 g) crème fraîche (see page 21) or sour cream
2   tablespoons snipped or chopped chives and/or parsley

① Preheat the oven to 375°F (190°C). Place a ½-inch (1-cm) layer of the kosher salt in the bottom of a roasting pan. Arrange the potatoes in a single layer over the salt and pour the remaining salt over the potatoes. Bake for 50 minutes, until easily pierced with the tip of a knife. Remove the potatoes from the oven and let stand for 10 minutes.

② Remove the potatoes from the pan and brush off any salt clinging to the potato skins. Halve the potatoes and season with salt and pepper. Drizzle the lemon juice over the potatoes. Lightly whip the crème fraîche or sour cream with a fork and drizzle it over the top, scatter with the chopped herbs, and serve.

> **LET'S DISH**
> Don't despair when you see the empty pan. There's an easy way to clean it: Simply pour boiling water into it, let it cool enough so you don't burn your fingers, then scrub.

SIDE DISHES

Honey-Orange Carrots

You can make this dish ahead of time, undercooking the carrots slightly and reheating it just before serving. Time on your hands? Time for a manicure.

Prep & cook time 25 min | Serves 4

½ **cup (120 ml) water or chicken broth**
2   **tablespoons unsalted butter**
1   **tablespoon honey**
Juice of 2 oranges, plus grated zest of 1 orange
2   **whole star anise**
2   **pounds (900 g) carrots, sliced diagonally**
Salt and ground black pepper

1. Set a large sauté pan over medium-high heat. Add the water or broth, butter, honey, orange juice and zest, and star anise to the pan and bring to a boil.

2. Add the carrots, reduce the heat to a gentle simmer, cover, and cook for about 5 minutes. Remove the lid and continue to cook for another 10–12 minutes, or until the liquid has turned to a glaze and the carrots are tender but firm. Season with salt and pepper to taste before serving.

> ## Swap It!
> Don't panic if star anise is missing from your spice rack. You can substitute 1–2 cinnamon sticks or 4–5 cloves. For a bit more spice, add 1 teaspoon of minced fresh ginger.

Caramelized Shallots

Once cooked, the skins slip off easily—it's fun to do as you eat.

Prep & cook time 1¼ hr | Serves 4–6

2   pounds (900g) shallots
2   tablespoons olive oil
2   tablespoons sherry or balsamic vinegar
Salt and ground black pepper

Preheat the oven to 425°F (220°C). Put the shallots with the remaining ingredients into a baking dish, and toss well to coat. Bake for 1 hour, turning once halfway through.

Creamy Greens with Onions

Go green! This dish will give you extra energy to stay out late!

Prep & cook time 20 min | Serves 4

2   tablespoons olive oil
3   tablespoons butter
4   medium red onions, sliced
Salt and ground black pepper
3   cups (200 g) chopped spinach or kale, ribs removed
½   cup (120 ml) cream

Heat a sauté pan over medium heat. Swirl in the oil and butter. When heated, add the onions and season with salt and pepper. Sauté 10 minutes, until the onion is soft. Stir in the greens and cook for 2–3 minutes, until wilted. Add the cream and cook for another 2–3 minutes before serving.

Drunken Pears

Serve these pears as they are, or for added decadence, with chocolate sauce or a slice of blue cheese. Drink enough wine with these, and you and your guy could be a drunken pair, too.

Prep & cook time, plus chilling time **50 min**   Serves 6

3   **cups (700 ml) red wine**
2   **cups (475 ml) water**
1   **cup (200 g) sugar**
1–2 cinnamon sticks
6   **firm Bosc pears, peeled, stems intact**

1 Put the wine, water, sugar, and cinnamon stick into a deep saucepan that's large enough to hold the pears snugly. Set the pot over medium-high heat and bring to a boil. Stir and reduce the heat to a gentle simmer.

2 Add the pears—they should be completely submerged. Cook, at a gentle simmer, for 30–40 minutes, or until just tender and easily pierced with a paring knife (the cooking time will vary, depending on the ripeness of the pears).

3 Transfer the pears to a dish and let cool. Continue simmering the liquid until it thickens enough to coat the back of a spoon. Add a splash of wine to brighten the flavor, if you like, and pour the syrup over the pears. Let the pears chill in the refrigerator for 3–4 hours before serving. They will last up to 5 days if refrigerated.

Swap It!
If you prefer white over red wine, use it instead, but toss in a ½-inch (1-cm) piece of fresh ginger for a spicy kick.

Turkish Oranges

The flavors are strong, the prep is easy, and everyone will be enchanted. What's not to like?

Prep & cook time, plus chilling time **20 min** | Serves 8

8	navel oranges
1½	cups (300 g) sugar
3	cups (700 ml) water
1	cinnamon stick
3–4 cloves
1	star anise

Heavy cream, lightly whipped, and a cookie to serve

1. Using a sharp paring knife, cut the tops and bottoms off the oranges so they stand upright on a cutting board. Peel the oranges, cutting down and around the flesh to remove the white pith along with the peel. Place the peeled oranges in an ovenproof dish.

2. In a saucepan, bring the sugar, water, cinnamon, cloves, and star anise to a boil. Simmer for 3–5 minutes, stirring occasionally, until the sugar has dissolved and the syrup is slightly thick.

3. Pour the hot syrup over the oranges and let cool. Cover and transfer to the refrigerator for at least 3 hours. Serve with a dollop of heavy cream and a cookie alongside.

DESSERTS

Speedy Chocolate Mousse

This chocolate mousse has all the sensual, indulgent properties of the real deal, but without the work or worry of using raw eggs. A make-ahead dessert with wow factor.

Prep & cook time, plus chilling time 15 min | Serves 8

9	**ounces (250 g) bittersweet or semisweet chocolate**
¼	**cup (60 ml) strong brewed coffee**
3	**tablespoons water**
1	**tablespoon sugar**
4	**tablespoons butter, cubed**
1	**cup (240 ml) heavy cream**

1 Put the chocolate, coffee, water, and sugar in a medium, microwave-safe bowl. Microwave at 20-second intervals, stirring after each interval, until the chocolate is just melted. Stir until completely smooth and add the butter. Stir again until the mixture is uniform and glossy.

2 In a separate bowl, using an electric mixer set on medium speed, beat the cream until it holds soft, drooping peaks.

3 Whisk one-third of the whipped cream into the melted chocolate. Then, in two additions, gently fold in the remaining cream until just combined and no white streaks remain. Spoon the chocolate-cream mixture into individual serving dishes and chill in the refrigerator for at least 3 hours before serving. (You can make it a day ahead.)

Choc-a-Berry Bread Pudding

Bread pudding is the stuff of cozy memories. With this easy recipe, you'll have more time at home—but not by the range!

Prep & cook time, plus chilling time 1¾ hr | Serves 8

1 **tablespoon butter**
5 **slices brioche (a butter-based bread) or good white bread**
3 **large eggs**
3 **egg yolks**
¼ **cup (50 g) sugar, plus extra for sprinkling**
1½ **cups (350 ml) heavy cream**
1½ **cups (350 ml) milk**
½ **teaspoon vanilla**
¼ **teaspoon salt**
10 **ounces (275 g) bittersweet chocolate, broken into pieces**
½ **pint (150 g) raspberries**

1 Preheat the oven to 350°F (180°C). Grease a medium baking dish with the butter. Stack the bread slices and cut them into quarters. In a large bowl, whisk together the eggs, yolks, and sugar. Add the cream, milk, vanilla, and salt and whisk until well combined.

2 Spread the chocolate across the bottom of the dish and lay the berries over it. Arrange the bread over the berries in a snug, single layer (overlap the bread, if needed). Pour the egg-cream mixture over the bread and press down so the bread is soaked. Top with a liberal sprinkling of sugar.

3 Place the baking dish in a larger roasting pan. Pour enough hot water into the pan so it comes halfway up the sides of the dish. Bake for 1 hour and 20 minutes, or until the pudding is set, golden, and puffed in the center. Serve warm or at room temperature.

Chocolate Dream Cake

This quick-and-easy chocolate-lover's cake will win over any crowd, any time. Finish it off with a scoop of ice cream, a chocolate sauce, or berries and cream—the choice is yours.

Prep & cook time 35 min | Serves 8

1 cup (2 sticks/200 g) butter, softened, plus extra for greasing
1 tablespoon unsweetened cocoa
9 ounces (250 g) 72% cocoa chocolate, broken into pieces
4 large eggs
2 cups (400 g) confectioners' sugar
½ cup (75 g) all-purpose flour, sifted
1 teaspoon vanilla
⅛ teaspoon salt
Ice cream to serve (optional)

1 Preheat the oven to 350°F (180°C) and set the rack in the center. Grease a 10-inch (25-cm) round cake pan with butter and dust the pan with the cocoa, tapping out any excess powder.

2 Put the chocolate and butter into a small microwave-safe bowl. Microwave at a high setting at 20-second intervals, stirring after each interval, until the chocolate has just melted. Do not overcook the chocolate. Stir the mixture until completely smooth and uniform. Set aside.

3 In a separate bowl, beat together the eggs and sugar. Stir in the flour, vanilla, and salt. Stir in the chocolate mixture until just combined.

4 Transfer the batter to the prepared cake pan and spread it out evenly. Bake in the preheated oven for

20–25 minutes, or until a toothpick inserted in the center emerges clean. Remove from the oven and set on a rack to cool. Serve with a scoop of ice cream.

VARIATION

QUICK CHOCOLATE SAUCE

Place 6 ounces (175 g) of bittersweet chocolate, broken into pieces, 2 tablespoons of sugar, and ⅛ teaspoon of salt into a microwave-safe bowl. Microwave on a high setting at 20-second intervals, stirring after each interval, until the chocolate is just melted. Do not overcook the chocolate. Stir in ¼ cup (60 ml) of cream until the sauce is completely smooth and uniform. Pour the sauce over the cake. You can refrigerate the sauce, covered, for 2 weeks.

BERRIES AND CREAM

Serve the cake with raspberries or sliced strawberries, to add color and temper the cake's richness, along with whipped cream. For strawberries, add a squeeze of lemon juice and a little sugar. Let sit until the berries release some of their juices. Toss and taste. Add more sugar or lemon juice, if needed.

For whipped cream, add ⅛ teaspoon of vanilla extract to 1 cup (240 ml) of heavy cream and whisk until soft peaks form when the whisk or beaters are lifted up. If you like yours sweet, add 1 tablespoon of sugar after the cream begins to thicken but before it holds soft peaks.

> **WHIP IT UP**
>
> When whipping cream, make sure you don't overbeat it or you'll lose the silky, smooth appeal. Always whip in a clean bowl and use a clean whisk or beaters. If you whisk by hand, first chill the bowl and the whisk in the freezer.

Light Menus

To make both the hedonist and the calorie counter happy, light meals need to be satisfying. The following meals are full of flavor—and your friends will be sated, not overstuffed.

THE PERFECT PICNIC

This menu will keep you cool as a cucumber on a hot summer's day, whether you eat at home or outdoors.

Cucumber-Avocado Soup page 109
Niçoise: Tout Simples page 75
Apricots Meet Vanilla page 100

HAVE A BALL WITH CHICKEN

Despite being healthy, this is so good that after every time I serve it, every plate is clean.

Baked Chicken Meatballs page 51
Brazen Broccoli page 61
Red Rice Royale page 74

COD WITH ASPARAGUS

Cod with olives and asparagus is healthy, flavorful, and filling. And the oranges give you a vitamin C boost.

Black Cod with Olive Relish page 55
Roasted Asparagus, Plain and Simple page 65
Turkish Oranges page 125

Midweek Menus

You're home and you're hungry. You can whip up a salad (served with crusty bread) or a main dish in Shop and serve! (pages 14–37), and dinner's done in under 30 minutes. Or let one of these menus inspire you, so you can spend even less time wandering around the kitchen.

SPICE UP THE NIGHT

Perfect for a winter's night when you want something spicy, delicious, and warm. And just so you don't starve waiting for the stew to finish simmering, there's No-Chop Guac to snack on.

No-Chop Guac page 19
Simply Stewed page 81
Couscous—Quick! Quick! page 37

DINNER IN A SNAP

A winning menu with plenty of good-for-you greens.

Instant Peanut Noodle Salad page 35
Snappy Peas page 92
Brazen Broccoli page 61

Sample menus

SHORT-ORDER SUPPER

Get the sweet potatoes ready and in the oven first, then prep the spinach. Do the omelet last, and it'll all be ready at the right time.

No-Flip Omelet page 71
Popeye Loves Olive Oil page 95
Roasted Sweet Potato Fries page 61

SIMPLY SATISFYING

This dinner is so easy, you'll even have time to make dessert.

Tri-Colored Salad page 25
Carbonara à la Kitty page 78
Berries with Honeyed Mascarpone page 98

ONE FOR THE MEAT-AND-POTATOES CREW

This is perfect for when you deserve a treat, but want to eat it in a hurry. Just be sure to put the tomatoes in the oven and the potatoes on to boil before you start making the steak.

Just-a-Few-Minutes Steak page 85
Smashed Red Potatoes page 94
Any-Thyme Tomatoes page 64

For the Family

I like to think of the table as a family gathering spot, and food the glue that holds it together. My secret? Make dishes that everyone enjoys but requires little time in the kitchen. These menus are sure to please—even if you're not a gourmet chef.

MEATLOAF MEETS TWO VEGGIES

Meatloaf is a classic enjoyed by grown-ups and children alike. Add some bacon and fabulous vegetables and everyone will get along.

Bacon Meatloaf page 50
Smashed Red Potatoes page 94
Honey-Orange Carrots page 122

THROW YOUR (MEXICAN) HAT INTO THE RING

Thanks to the braised pork carnitas, dinnertime turns into a fun tacos party. I cover my table with a selection of dishes—tortillas, carnitas, taco garnishes, and sides—giving everyone a chance to choose what they want without the typical "I don't like that" complaints.

No-Chop Guac page 19
Blame It on the Pretty Pork Carnitas pages 44–45
Jalapeño-Butter Corn page 93

Sample menus

FAST (AND FUN) FOOD

This is not your typical fast-food burger and fries—make the turkey burger variation and you'll have a meal trimmed of fat. However, your family won't mind—this food is full of flavor. Peanut butter cookies end the night on just the right note.

Burger Bonanza pages 82–83
Roasted Sweet Potato Fries page 61
Peanut Butter and Choc page 105

BARELY BROKE A SWEAT BBQ

Peach salad kicks off this summertime BBQ. To keep those summer whites clean, supply plenty of napkins with the finger-licking ribs.

Peach and Mozzarella Salad page 27
Ribs Extra page 52
Molasses Baked Beans page 57
Chocolate Chip Cookies page 103

IT'S A SNAP CHICKEN DINNER

Who doesn't love a good chicken dinner? Of course, choose only one of the options for the roast chicken. The bread pudding is a cozy finale for cold winter nights.

Roast Chicken, Four Ways pages 48–49
Snappy Peas page 92
Polenta (aka Grits) page 119
Choc-a-Berry Bread Pudding page 127

Meatless Meals

To make a meal that suits vegetarians and meat eaters alike, I consider every course. In each of these menus, the dishes combine to make a complete meal. Satisfying both vegetarians and carnivores at the table is an essential part of modern-day entertaining. I think these menus do just that. So there.

GO WILD!

Earthy mushrooms complement the sweet tomatoes and creamy baked ricotta. The cake (an indulgent finale if there ever was one) is delicous served at room temperature.

Roasted Mushrooms with Garlic and Parsley page 40
Baked Ricotta page 59
Any-Thyme Tomatoes page 64
Chocolate Dream Cake pages 128–29

VEGETARIAN MENU, ITALIAN STYLE

This sophisticated vegetarian meal, my nod to Italy, is both luxurious and satisfying. Have the crostini ready and the risotto waiting in the oven. Bellissimo!

My Favorite Crostini page 20
Take-a-Break Pea Risotto page 118
Baked Figs with Mascarpone page 99

Sample menus

SPICE IT UP, MIDDLE-EASTERN STYLE

Flavors from the Middle East are sumptuous and robust. I always find that the spicy aromas add an extra dimension to this simple meal.

Zesty Olives page 16
Chickpea Mash page 36
Winter-Warming Veggies page 67
Turkish Oranges page 125

DOWN-HOME COMFORT FOOD

My bread pudding is a filling main dish, and the greens will add color to the plate. The dip begins the meal right and the pears bring it home.

Go Dippy page 18
Savory Bread Pudding page 42
Creamy Greens with Onions page 123
Drunken Pears page 124

EVERYONE'S FAVORITE: MAC AND CHEESE

My outrageously delicious mac and cheese needs a refreshing appetizer and a tasty side. The cookies add a twist suitable for the nostalgic main course.

Tri-Colored Salad page 25
Unforgettable Mac and Cheese page 56
Popeye Loves Olive Oil page 95
Ebony and Ivory Cookies page 104

Life's too short to chop onions

Entertaining

Entertaining can be anything but. To minimize any anxiety, these luxurious dishes can all be made or partially prepared in advance. There's no need to get them on the plate at an exact time—so don't panic if you're not ready when the timer goes off. Who knows? You may even find entertaining entertaining.

SUMPTUOUS STEAK DINNER

A meal for meat eaters. Make the soup and corn ahead of time, and reheat before serving. Prepare the crumble ahead, and put it in the oven before sitting down for the main dish.

Classic Potato Leek Soup page 73
Bistro Pepper Steak with Blue Cheese page 115
Jalapeño-Butter Corn page 93
Peachy Granola Crumble page 101

MAKE-AHEAD CHICKEN

Prepare the mousse a day in advance. Make the polenta and chicken hours ahead and reheat before serving. About 15 minutes before the guests arrive, stick the Camembert in the oven. Just concentrate on keeping the wine glasses full.

Camembert in a Box page 108
Chicken Legs with Cream and Leeks page 112
Polenta (aka Grits) page 119
Speedy Chocolate Mousse page 126

138_

Sample menus

MY PERFECT DINNER PARTY

Each dish has notable flavors, yet each needs only simply prepared ingredients. I normally marinate the lamb the day before. Early on the day I make the spinach and prepare the crab salad (assembling the salad 15 minutes prior to serving).

No-Cook Crab Salad page 110
My Mom's Lamb Roast page 116
Salt-Roasted Potatoes page 121
Creamy Greens with Onions page 123

LAMB, TUNISIAN STYLE

All these dishes can be made hours or even a day in advance. Reheat the lamb and couscous before serving. I let the goat cheese and pears come to room temperature by setting them out at least 30 minutes ahead of time.

Goat Cheese to Go page 19
Luscious Lamb Stew page 88
Couscous—Quick! Quick! page 37
Drunken Pears page 124

STRESS-FREE DUCK FEAST

Make the duck and tart hours ahead of time. Serve the duck at room temperature but reheat the figs. I keep the figs and shallots in a warm oven while everyone enjoys a cocktail.

Figs Gone A-Fowl page 114
Caramelized Shallots page 123
Winnning Wild Rice page 120
Pass-It-On Apricot Tart page 102

Index

Index

Index

Index

Index

ACKNOWLEDGMENTS

The author would like to give a special thanks to the invaluable Julie Randolph. Thank you for all your work and support in testing, eating, and all that went with and beyond. She'd also like to thank Papa Greenwald, Aunt Jane, Ava, Diana, other members and friends of the Greenwald clan, Theresa Bebbington, Ellen Dupont, and the Montalvo Arts Center, Saratoga, California, which graciously allowed her to test recipes during her residency, along with all the artists and friends that tasted trials (both good and not so good) along the way.